M GASPAR LEFEBVRE O.

HOW TO UNDERSTAND THE MASS

ILLUSTRATIONS BY
JOS. SPEYBROUCK

Catholic Authors Press
www.CatholicAuthors.com

NIHIL OBSTAT :
Brugis, 14 Aprilis 1954,
Fr. Archangelus a Reg. Carm. O.C.D., libr. cens.

IMPRIMATUR :
Brugis, 15 Aprilis 1954.
M. De Keyzer, vic. gen.

IMPRIMI POTEST :
die 16 Aprilis 1954.
† Theodorus Nève, Abbas Sti Andreæ.

First published in 1937
This edition published 2006

ISBN: 0-9789432-6-0

Copyright 2006 Catholic Authors Press
www.CatholicAuthors.com

TABLE OF CONTENTS

Introduction: What is a Sacrifice?	1
Preparation in the sacristy	8
Entrance to the altar	11
Division of the Mass	13
Analysis of the Mass	14

I. — MASS OF THE CATECHUMENS : PRAYER AND TEACHING

1st PART: PREPARATORY PRAYERS *(At the foot of the altar)*

Sign of the Cross	16
1. *Judica*	17
2. Confiteor	19
3. Going up to the altar	22

2nd PART: PRAYERS AND READINGS *(From Introit to Offertory)*

4. Introit	27
5. *Kyrie eleison*	28
6. *Gloria in excelsis*	31
7. Collect	34
8. Epistle	37
9. Gradual. 10. *Munda Cor*	40 to 42
11. Gospel	43
12. Credo	46

II. — MASS OF THE FAITHFUL: SACRIFICE AND COMMUNION

1st PART: PREPARATION OF THE SACRIFICE *(From Offertory to Preface)*

13. Offertory Antiphon	49
14. *Suscipe Sancte Pater*: Oblation of the host without stain	49
15. *Deus qui humanæ*: The fusion of wine and water	53
16. *Offerimus tibi*: Oblation of the chalice of salvation	54
17. *In spiritu*. 18. *Veni Sanctificator*. 19. *Lavabo*: Prayers and purification	57 to 59
20. *Suscipe Sancta Trinitas*: Honour to God and to His Saints	60
21. *Orate fratres*. 22. Secret: Conclusion of the Offertory	63

V

2nd PART: CONSUMMATION OF THE SACRIFICE *(From Preface to Pater Noster)*

23. Preface. 24. *Sanctus.* 25. *Benedictus*: Prelude to the Eucharistic Prayer . . . . 66 to 71
26. *Te igitur.* 27. *1st Memento* (Living). 28. *Communicantes*: Prayer for the Church on earth . . . . 72 to 75
29. *Hanc igitur.* 30. *Quam oblationem*: May God accomplish the Transubstantiation . . . . 75 to 77
31. *Qui pridie*: Transubstantiation of the bread into the Body of Jesus . 77 to 81
32. *Simili modo*: Transubstantiation of the wine into the Blood of Jesus . 81 to 83
33. *Unde et memores*: Oblation of the Victim sacramentally immolated . 83 to 85
34. *Supra quæ.* 35. *Supplices*: Acceptance of the Victim by God . 86 to 89
36. *2nd Memento* (Dead): Application of the Sacrifice to the Church suffering . . . . 89 to 91
37. *Nobis quoque peccatoribus*: Application of the Sacrifice to the Church militant . . . . 92 to 94
38. *Per quem.* 39. *Per Ipsum*: Conclusion of the Eucharistic Prayer . 95 to 97

3rd PART: PARTICIPATION IN THE SACRIFICE *(From Pater Noster to end)*

40. The Lord's Prayer: *Pater noster* . . . . 98 to 100
41. *Libera nos.* 42. Breaking of Bread. 43. *Pax Domini* . . . 101 to 103
44. Mingling. 45. *Agnus Dei.* 46. Prayer before the Kiss of peace . 104 to 106
47. Prayers before Communion. 48. *Domine non sum dignus.* 49. Communion. 50. Ablutions . . . . 107 to 112
51. Communion Antiphon. 52. Postcommunion. 53. *Ite missa est.* 54. *Placeat.* 55. Blessing . . . . 113 to 115
56. Last Gospel (St John) . . . . 116 to 118
57. Prayers after Mass. — Departure . . . . 119 to 121

INTRODUCTION

WHAT IS A SACRIFICE

NECESSITY OF SACRIFICE IN GENERAL

Man, owing entire dependence on God in both the natural and supernatural order, must acknowledge and honour him as his sovereign Lord and Father, must ask of him the help and graces that he needs, and thank him for all those benefits, temporal and spiritual, that he unceasingly bestows.

Sacrifice, the supreme exercise of the virtue of religion, reserved to God alone, has in all times been the means by which man, more or less perfectly indeed, fulfilled this threefold duty of adoration, thanksgiving and petition. But since the fall of Adam the whole human race is bound to offer sacrifice to God to propitiate him and obtain his forgiveness.

NECESSITY OF THE SACRIFICE OF THE MAN-GOD ON THE ALTAR OF CALVARY

Alone a man-God could in complete justice make up for the offence given to God by the proud refusal of obedience on the part of our first father and by the sins of all men, his descendants. And God, in his unlimited mercy sent his own Son into the world to take flesh in the womb of the blessed Virgin Mary and to become thereby the high Priest of humanity and its one propitiatory mediator. « For we have not, » says St Paul, « a high priest, who cannot have compassion on our infirmities : but one tempted in all things like as we are, without sin » (*Hebrews 4, 15*). « God, sending his own Son in the likeness of sinful flesh » (*Rom. 8, 3*) that is mortal, determined that the incarnate Word, who ought to have had an immortal human nature, should take on the responsibility of sinful humanity, and, by undergoing death, which for all men is the punishment for original sin, should deliver them from spiritual death and obtain for them one day to share in his resurrection, that is in the immortality of his body.

The incarnate Word, then, for love of us, of his own will gave himself up to the agents of him who had become « the prince of this world » (*John 14, 30*) because he had brought our first parents under his sway; Christ, by allowing these agents to nail him to the cross and to shed all his Blood, offered himself to his Father as a victim of infinite reparation.

By this heroic act of love and obedience his was the right to lead all men back to God, since he had superabundantly paid their debt and had obtained for them all the grace of which they stood in need to be delivered from sin and Satan and return, like the Prodigal Son, to their heavenly Father.

CALVARY FULFILS THE ESSENTIAL CONDITIONS OF A TRUE SACRIFICE

Sacrifice is defined as follows: 1) Sacrifice, in the proper meaning of the word, is an act of exterior worship by which man, under the sign of a visible offering, signifies the interior act of religion by which he acknowledges the supreme dominion of God and the total dependence of man on God and submits himself to him: 2) hence sacrifice is an expression of adoration, thanksgiving, petition and atonement and 3) is offered in order to effect a closer union with God.

1) *Exterior and interior worship offered to God*

In order that there may be sacrifice by man, who is a social being made up of body and soul, a *visible* action carried out by a priest in the name of the whole of society must be the exterior interpretation of the interior worship of adoration, thanksgiving, petition and reparation that souls make to God.

This was fully effected on Calvary which was the most striking and palpable testimony offered in the spirit of the purest love and obedience to the rights of God's holiness and justice in order to reconcile all sinners with him.

The incarnate Word, the Head of all human society, gave to his Father the spiritual homage of dependence due to him from all men, by dying on the cross as he prayed aloud, « Father, forgive them » (*Luke 23*, 34). « Jesus cried with a loud voice, saying: ...My God, my God, why hast thou forsaken me? » (*Ps. 21*, 1; *Matth. 27*, 46). « And Jesus crying with a loud voice, said: Father, into thy hands I commend my spirit. And saying this, he gave up the ghost. » (*Ps. 30*, 6; *Luke 23*, 46) For the whole of this time Jesus allowed his Blood to flow, literally, drop by drop — a very real symbol of love — and to cause him to suffer a burning thirst to which he gave expression by saying: *Sitio* (I thirst) (*John 19*, 28). This cry shows, too, how his divine heart burned with the desire to save souls. *Sitit sitiri*, says St Augustine.

Never was a death more ignominious or painful, but it provided the man-God with the occasion of practising virtue to a heroic degree.

2) *The four ends of sacrifice*

The sacrifice of the Cross was a propitiatory sacrifice; that is its specific character. Jesus had warned his apostles when he told them on the night before, at the Last Supper, as he gave them the consecrated bread and wine to eat and drink: « This is my body which shall be *delivered* — *tradetur* — for you » (*I Cor. 11*, 24); « This is my blood..., which *shall be shed* — *effundetur* — for many unto the remission of sins » (*Matth. 26*, 28): *the blood which is shed* is the counterpart of the expression the *body delivered* or *immolated*. These two elements are the two aspects of one and the same sacrifice: the blood issues from the body immolated on the cross.

This sacrifice, accompanied with the shedding of blood, which for Jesus consisted in offering through love and amidst tremendous sufferings, his infinitely precious life in reparation for our sins, earned pardon for them by satisfying divine justice.

The sacrifice of the cross was also a sacrifice of adoration, thanksgiving and petition, for these are generic features of every sacrifice. By working to make reparation to divine honour outraged by sin Jesus acknowledged God's sovereign majesty and the blessings bestowed by him on man. In addition he showed clearly that he desired to reconcile us with his Father and, in consequence, that mankind expected of him the indispensable means of obtaining this reconciliation and of remaining in that state.

3) *Union of man with God*

Since he was God, Jesus could escape his executioners and prevent death having any dominion over him. Therefore, the shedding of his Blood, accepted voluntarily, which was both the sign and one of the principal causes of his death, showed at the same time the new Adam's desire to make expiation for the betrayal by the old Adam whose mortal body he had inherited for this end.

By this heroic offering of human-divine life he ensured for Adam and all his descendants the new life of complete submission to God of which his resurrection is the pattern, the pledge and the instrument. « *By his death,* » we sing in the Easter Preface, « *he overcame our death, and by rising again restored our life* » (Cf. *Romans 4,* 25).

This reconciliation with God by the death, with blood shedding, of our Saviour was foretold to the company of the apostles when at the Last Supper the divine Master spoke of the new covenant that was to take the place of the old. In former days, after the victims were sacrificed, Moses poured out half of their blood over the altar, which represented God, while with the other half he sprinkled the people and in this way sealed the covenant made by Yahweh with Israel (*Exod.* 24, 5-8).

The new and definitive covenant, which the old merely prepared and foreshadowed, was in the same manner ratified in blood, in divine blood, in the blood which the man-God shed when he was immolated, a true Paschal Lamb, on the cross. Moreover, as the new Moses, Jesus, speaking to his twelve apostles, as Moses spoke to the twelve tribes of Israel, gave them the chalice saying: « Drink ye all of this ; for this is my blood of the new testament, which shall be shed for many unto the remission of sins. And I say to you, I will not drink from henceforth of this fruit of the vine until that day when I shall drink it with you new in the kingdom of my Father » (*Matth.* 26, 27-29).

The sacrifice, with shedding of blood, of the cross has thus thrown open to us the heavenly kingdom where, for all eternity, God will make us drink of a new wine, the wine of divine love.

THE EUCHARISTIC SACRIFICE

« And this day shall be for a memorial to you, » God said to his people by the mouth of Moses, speaking of the old, figurative passover, « and you shall keep it a feast to the Lord in your generations with an everlasting observance » (*Exod. 12,* 14). Jesus did likewise for the real pasch, the divine victim of our altars, for before he died he instituted the Eucharist in the form of a sacrificial meal so that by offering and partaking of the bread and wine consecrated to be his Body and Blood we might be joined to the victorious sacrifice of Calvary, that is to Christ's victory of which Mass is the memorial and the most efficacious realisation.

By effecting the transubstantiation, with two different and successive consecratory formulas, of the *bread* into his Body : « *This is my body,* » and of the *wine* into his Blood : « *This is the chalice of my blood* », Jesus really offered himself as a victim to his Father by an exterior rite which designated the offering, with blood shedding, of Calvary, which for this reason is called an immolation. This rite of oblation, without blood shedding, was the sacrament or sign, of the Passion which was to take place the next day, and that explains the essential unity existing between the Eucharistic sacrifice and that of the cross. It is the same sacrifice for it is the same priest who offers the same Victim, that is, Jesus, but in two different ways of which Calvary alone wrought our redemption.

The High-Priest of the new law, then, having himself celebrated the first Eucharistic sacrifice, foretold by Melchisedech's offering of bread and wine (*Genesis 14*, 18), commanded his Church to celebrate it after him. The Council of Trent adds, indeed, that « Jesus at this moment instituted as priests of the New Testament the apostles and their successors in the priesthood, and *commanded* them to offer by these words : Do this for a commemoration of me » (Sess. 22, c. 1).

Contrary to the rites of immolation and pouring out of the blood of animals in the temple of Jerusalem, which were merely a foreshadowing of the future immolation of the divine Victim and of the shedding of his Blood on the cross, the ritual immolation of the Mass is a figure of the death of Jesus, which has now taken place, and is so by making him present in person in the state of a victim on our altars by means of the two formulas of consecration which are said one over the bread and the other over the wine. These formulas, which possess a special efficacy, correspond with what they signify and produce *two different* effects by virtue of which *the bread,* for a special reason, is the *sacramental sign* or the *sacrament of the Body* and *the wine,* the *sacramental sign* or the sacrament of the *Saviour's Blood,* although in fact Christ is whole and entire under each of the two Eucharistic species. This twofold sacramental signification, which corresponds with the two entirely distinct transubstantiations or miraculous conversions, enables it to be said in all truth that it is especially the Body and Blood of Jesus which are offered under the species of bread and wine ; and that this offering of the Body and Blood, thus sacramentally separated, renews, without blood shedding but very significantly, the offering of Calvary itself. In fact it *makes present* on the altar the Lamb of God who is in a state of « perpetual Victim » in heaven (St Thomas, IV Dist. 12, exp. lit) and, by effecting it in a sacramental and very real manner, represents the shedding of his Blood which occurred on Calvary.

The Mass, in which in this way the divine Victim is offered by a rite of visible immolation, that is by a sacramental rite which is essentially representative of his death with the shedding of blood on the cross, and which, like it, is the expression of the interior charity and obedience with which our Saviour offered himself on the altar of the Cross, possesses therefore all the constituent elements of a real sacrifice, but without shedding of blood.

Priests through whom the Church offers this sacrifice, *ab Ecclesia per sacerdotes immolandum* (Con. Trident. Ss 22, c. 1), act as ministers and instruments of Christ since it is by the words of consecration, said by the priest, that God effects the great marvel of the twofold transubstantiation. It is therefore the high Priest of the Last Supper and of Calvary who, invisibly by divine power and visibly by the external ministry of the priest, continues unceasingly everyday throughout the world (there are upwards of 300,000 Masses daily) the oblation which he himself made on the cross in order to apply its fruits to mankind and thus to bring them ever increasingly nearer to God.

Far from detracting from the one sacrifice at which, once for all, our redemption was achieved, Mass is an affirmation of its unique worth. It is Calvary, and consequently the infinite adoration, thanksgiving, petition and reparation of Golgotha which in it are offered to God in order that he may look favourably upon us.

The Eucharistic sacrifice, the replica of Calvary, re-iterates the offering there made, by placing the Victim, formerly blood-stained and now immortal for ever, under the sacramental sign of a bloodless body and of blood poured out, as is clearly shown by the juxtaposition of the bread and wine respectively called by Christ at the Last Supper, and frequently by the celebrant at Mass, *corpus et sanguis*.

« If, at the consecration, shedding of blood is mentioned, » says the Roman Catechism, « it is because in that way the Passion of our Saviour is better expressed, for in it the Blood was separated from the Body » (XIX, 2). « The Blood, consecrated separately, places before the eyes of all in a far more forceful and efficacious manner, the Passion of our Lord, his death and the nature of his sufferings » (XVIII, 3).

Christ instituted the sacrament of the Eucharist in this way and Canon Law forbids, even in a case of urgent necessity, its being done otherwise than by consecrating bread and wine, for our Saviour commanded it to be done as he did it (Canon 817).

HOW TO UNDERSTAND THE MASS explains this teaching in detail and endeavours to show how the Church effects at the altar this sacrificial and propitiatory enactment of the Redemption in the Blood of Christ in such a way as to ensure its greatest possible efficacy.

COLLECT FOR CORPUS CHRISTI

No better conclusion for this introduction may be found than to quote the collect of the Mass of Corpus Christi, composed by the angelic Doctor. In it the Church alludes to both the Body and Blood of Christ. In this way she asserts the unity of the sacrament of the Eucharist, while taking into consideration the two elements « the bread and the wine which constitute its integral matter » (Roman Catechism, XVIII, 2).

« O God, who in this wonderful sacrament hast left us a memorial of thy Passion, grant us, we beseech thee, so to reverence the sacred mysteries of thy Body and Blood, that we may ever perceive within us the fruit of thy redemption. »

IN THE SACRISTY : 1. The amice, spread out (below) and round the neck of the priest. — 2. The alb, made of linen or hemp. — 3. The girdle. — 4. 5. 6. The maniple, stole and chasuble, made of silk : the colour varying according to the day. — 7. The black biretta. — 8. The surplice. — 9. The purificator on the chalice. — 10. The chalice, the paten, the host and the pall. — 11. The veil for the chalice and the burse, made of silk like the vestments. — 12. The corporal, unfolded. — 13. The cruets. — 14. The lavabo towel for wiping the priest's hands. — 15. The ciborium.

PRELIMINARIES BEFORE MASS.

« Since human nature » says the Council of Trent, « does not easily lift itself to the meditation of divine things without some outside help, our good Mother the Church, in conformity with the discipline and the tradition of the Apostles, has established certain rites and made use of ceremonies : blessings, lights, incense, priestly vestments and numerous other similar means, to bring out the majesty of the Divine Sacrifice and to incite the spirit of the faithful to lift itself through these exterior signs of religion and piety to the contemplation of the sublime mysteries which lie hidden therein. » *(De Sacrificio Missae*, SS. XXII and XIIth Canon).

We shall seek, then, to gain an insight into what is said and done at the altar, for active participation in liturgical worship, centred on the Mass, is the means of glorifying God and of attaining to personal holiness.

PREPARATION IN THE SACRISTY.

In the sacristy, the priest begins by *washing his hands* and while he is doing this, he asks « to be able to serve God without defilement of mind or body ».

The *holy water* with which we sign ourselves when entering a church has a similar aim.

Next, the celebrant prepares the chalice, which Optatus of Milevum calls « the Bearer of the Blood of Jesus Christ ». He places on it the *purificator* which is used, as its name indicates, to purify the chalice and the fingers of the priest (No 9). The *paten* which is used for the offering of the bread, and « for the breaking and distribution of the Body of the Lord » (words of the Bishop when consecrating it) (No. 10). The *Host*, pure white and unbroken (No, 10). The *pall*, a piece of blessed linen, once the edge of the corporal « with which the Body and Blood of our Lord Jesus Christ were covered and enveloped » (formula for the blessing of the corporal) (No. 10). The silk *chalice veil* and the *burse* (No. 11) and in this burse, the *corporal*, folded into nine equal squares, which the Church calls « the new shroud for the Body of Jesus Christ », from which it gets its name corporal (No. 12).

The *ciborium* filled with hosts (No. 15), the *cruets* containing wine and water (No. 13) and the *finger* or « *lavabo* » *towel* (No. 14) have been prepared beforehand.

Then the celebrant vests himself with what the *Caeremoniale Episcoporum* calls « the sacred vestments » (l. II, c. 1 n. 4). They have all been blessed and have a symbolical meaning which is expressed in the prayer said as each is put on. The *amice*, put on the head and then round the neck, is « the helmet of salvation which helps to repel the temptations of the devil » (No. 1). The *alb* covers the whole body and represents « the whiteness of the soul which the Blood of the Lamb has purified » (No. 2). The *girdle*, tied round the waist, is « a girdle of purity which extinguishes the ardour of our passions » (No. 3). The silk *maniple*, worn on the left arm, and once meant to wipe sweat from the forehead, indicates that « through tears and suffering is the reward of labour merited » (No. 4). The *stole*, also of silk and crossed over the chest, is a sign of the priesthood and symbolizes « the robe of immortality lost by our first father » and won back again for us by Jesus (No. 5). Lastly, the *chasuble*, in which there is an opening for the priest to pass his head through, as if it were a yoke, and which entirely covers him, is « the easy yoke and the light burden of the Lord », for this wide vestment « symbolizes charity » (Ordination of a priest) (No. 6). The *biretta* replaces as a head covering the hood or the amice (No. 7). The *surplice* of the server is a diminished alb, and, like it, is a symbol of purity (No. 8).

Participating in the action of the priest, the faithful should share his dispositions.

We may add that to do needlework or any other work for the altar is also a way of participating in the Mass, and a means of obtaining the graces of which it is the source.

ENTRANCE TO THE ALTAR.

The server carrying the missal (if it is not already on the altar) and the priest carrying the chalice *(inset)* go to the altar for the holy Sacrifice.

In the middle of the altar stands a large crucifix, surrounded with candles of honour. This crucifix is to remind one of Calvary, for at Mass the Church preaches « Jesus, and Him crucified » (I Cor. II) and repeats in an unbloody manner the oblation of the Cross.

« The priesthood of Christ », says the Council of Trent, « was not meant to die at His death. Therefore, at the Last Supper, on the night in which He was betrayed, He left to His Church, His beloved spouse, a visible sacrifice, such as our nature needed : a sacrifice *which should represent the bloody sacrifice* which was about to be accomplished once for all on the cross ; *which would preserve the memory of it* until the end of the world, and *which would apply to us its saving virtue* in remission of the sins which we commit every day... In the divine sacrifice which is accomplished at Mass is contained and immolated (and hence offered) in an unbloody manner the same Christ Who in a bloody way offered Himself once on the altar of the Cross. This sacrifice is thus really propitiatory ». (Ss. XXII).

To attend Mass is to unite ourselves with Jesus Who presents at the altar to God, through the ministry of the priest, the same Blood which He shed on the Cross ; it is to take part in Calvary, which is always carried on by the same High Priest, Who offers always the same and only Victim, « *una eademque Hostia* » (Ss. XXII) Whose oblation alone is fully accepted.

Since the Eucharistic sacrifice and the sacrifice on Golgotha is essentially « *unum atque idem sacrificium* » (one and the same sacrifice), who does not see the enormous importance which lies in its celebration, and in having it celebrated or in attending and taking the greatest possible part in it ? « We are obliged to realize » says the same Council, « that Christians can accomplish nothing as holy and as divine as these wonderful mysteries in which the life-giving Victim, Who reconciles us with God the Father, is daily immolated by the priest at the altar ». (Ss. XXII).

ENTRANCE TO THE ALTAR: *(Top)* Jesus in the Synagogue at Nazareth (Luke IV, 16-29). — *(Altar and inset)* Two candles are lighted, or more for solemn occasions. The priest carrying the chalice and preceded by the server goes to the altar. — The Mass is offered by the Church, that our souls should actually benefit from the merits of Jesus on the Cross (large crucifix).

This oblation made by Jesus and the Church is of infinitely greater importance than all other acts of worship, infinitely greater than all actions, even the most heroic, of the saints, for all those prayers, all those virtues, all those merits, when they are put together, are limited, while those of Calvary are superabundant. If we do not benefit from them as we should, that is solely the fault of our dispositions; for the participation of the Holy Sacrifice requires the spirit of sacrifice, which is that of our Leader. *Sancta sanctis (see inset)*: holy things demand holiness, say the Eastern liturgies at the moment of Communion. And nothing is more efficacious in giving us these dispositions than our intimate unity with the celebrant, the minister of the Church.

When he arrives at the altar, the priest places on it the chalice on the corporal which he has spread out. Then he prepares the missal, which is placed on the missal stand on the right hand side. We follow his example and prepare ours before Mass.

DIVISION OF THE MASS.

We devote the next two pages (14 and 15) to the order of the Mass. It is divided into two main stages: the *Mass of the Catechumens*, (for the aspirants to baptism used to be present), and, beginning with the Offertory, the *Mass of the Faithful*.

The *Mass of the Catechumens* has for its origin the religious service which the people, under the Law of Moses, celebrated in the Synagogues. There were prayers, reading and explanation of the Scriptures, and singing of the Psalms. St. Luke tells us how Jesus read and explained at Nazareth a text from Isaias *(picture at the top)*. The Apostles carried on these reunions and made them Christian when they left the Synagogue.

The *Mass of the Faithful* is the renewal of the sacrificial banquet of the Last Supper, which Jesus substituted for that of the figurative Lamb instituted by Moses 1500 years earlier.

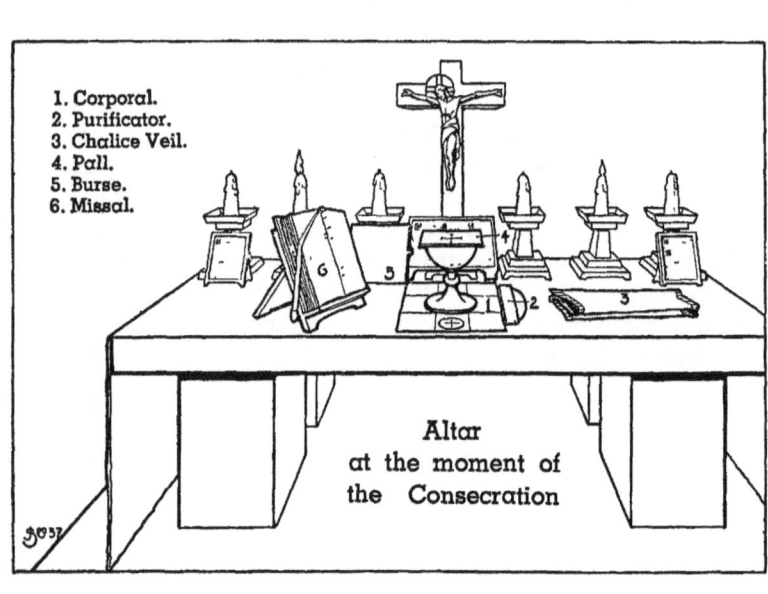

1. Corporal.
2. Purificator.
3. Chalice Veil.
4. Pall.
5. Burse.
6. Missal.

Altar at the moment of the Consecration

I. MASS OF THE CATECHUMENS.

PRAYERS : Man speaks to God — God speaks to man : READINGS.

1st Part: PREPARATORY PRAYERS (At foot of altar)	Gospel Side	(Entrance) 1 *Judica me*	Epistle Side
		2 *Confiteor*	
		3 Going up to altar	

2nd Part: PRAYERS AND READINGS (From Introit to Offertory)			4 Introit
		5 *Kyrie*	
		6 *Gloria in excelsis*	
			7 Collect
			8 Epistle
			9 Gradual All
		10 *Munda Cor*	
	11 Gospel		
		12 Credo	

II. MASS OF THE FAITHFUL.

SACRIFICE: Man gives himself to God. - God gives Himself to man: COMMUNION

1st Part : **PREPARATION OF THE SACRIFICE** *(Offertory to Preface)*	Gospel Side	13 Offertory - 14 *Suscipe* : Oblation of the Host	Epistle Side
			15 *Deus qui*
		16 *Offerimus* : Oblation of Chalice	
		17 *In spiritu* - 18 *Veni sanctificator*	
			19 *Lavabo*
		20 *Suscipe Sancta Trinitas*	
		21 *Orate Fratres* - 22 Secret	
2nd Part : **CONSUMMATION OF THE SACRIFICE** *(Preface to Pater noster)*		23 Preface	
		24 *Sanctus* - 25 *Benedictus*	
		26 *Te igitur*	
		27 Memento of Living - 28 *Communicantes*	
		29 *Hanc igitur* - 30 *Quam oblationem*	
		31 *Qui pridie*: Transubstantiation of the bread	
		32 *Simili modo* · Transubstantiation of the wine	
		33 *Unde et memores* - 34 *Supra* - 35 *Supplices*	
		36 Memento of Dead - 37 *Nobis quoque*	
		38 *Per quem* - 39 *Per ipsum*	
3rd Part : **PARTICIPATION IN THE SACRIFICE** *(Pater noster to end)*		40 *Pater noster* - 41 *Libera nos*	
		42 Breaking of Bread - 43 *Pax Domini*	
		44 Mingling - 45 *Agnus* - 46 *Domine Jesu*	
		47 Prayers bef Comm - 48 *Dne n. s. dignus*	
		49 Communion	50 Ablutions
			51 Ant Com.
			52 Postcomm.
		53 *Ite missa est* - 54 *Placeat* - 55 Blessing	
	56 Last Gospel	57 Prayers after Mass (Departure)	

JUDICA ME: *(Top)* A Levite in exile begs God to let him return to the Temple at Jerusalem, for he has no joy outside the service of his Lord. — *(Altar and inset)* The priest says: *In nomine Patris*, etc, for God is the beginning and the end of all our acts; and he traces on himself the Sign of the Redemption because it is by the Cross that God saves us and we go to God. The server, according to the general rule, is on the opposite side to the Missal, when this is open.

I. MASS OF THE CATECHUMENS

I. PREPARATORY PRAYERS : *At the foot of the Altar.*

1. PSALM 42 : JUDICA ME.
See illustration, p. 16.

The celebrant begins Mass by making the sign of the Cross *(inset)* :

In nomine.. *In the name of the Father, and of the Son, and of the Holy Ghost. Amen.*

Then he recites Psalm 42 : *Judica*, which was chosen for its fourth verse : *Introibo ad altare Dei*, which is used as an antiphon before and after *(picture of altar)*.

The server, and, if possible, the congregation, answer the priest. The prayer of the Church is nearly always in the form of a dialogue, so that the faithful can be more closely associated with it. This vocal participation creates a great unity between souls.

The Psalm *Judica* was composed by a Levite exiled far from Jerusalem, who wanted to return to sing once again the praises in the Temple. The Psalmist turns to God, Whose Name he insistently repeats *(Deus, Deus meus)* even as many as eight times; and he begs Him to take his cause in hand and to deliver him, by a just judgment, from the wicked and impious men among whom he is living, who are oppressing him *(picture at the top)*.

But why be discouraged ? God will come to his help and will let him return to Jerusalem. Then he will be able to climb the holy hill where stands the tabernacle *(tabernacula* [pural] for there are three precincts), and approach the altar of sacrifice and sing Psalms as he accompanies himself on the harp. This contact with God will fill him with a holy joy.

Antiphon : **Introibo**... *I will go in unto the Altar of God.*

R/ *Unto God, Who giveth joy to my youth.*

Psalm : V/ **Judica me**... *Judge me, O God, and plead my cause* *against an ungodly nation: O deliver me from the unjust and deceitful man.*

R/ *For Thou, O God, art my strength: why dost Thou cast me off? and why go I mourning, because of the oppression of the enemy?*

V/ *O send out Thy light and Thy truth: let them lead me and bring me unto Thine holy hill, and unto Thy tabernacles!*

R/ *Then will I go unto the Altar of God, unto God, the gladdener of my youth!*

V/ *Upon the harp will I praise Thee, O God, my God! Why are thou cast down, O my soul? and why dost thou disquiet me?*

R/ *Hope thou in God; for I will still praise Him, Who is the health of my countenance, and my God.*

V/ *Glory be to the Father, and to the Son, and to the Holy Ghost.*

R/ *As it was in the beginning, is now, and ever shall be, world without end. Amen.*

Antiphon: V/ *I will go in unto the Altar of God.*

R/ *Unto God, Who giveth joy to my youth.*

Exiled on this earth, let us too lift up our eyes to the holy hill, to the altar which is in a *high* place and ready for the sacrifice. For, in intimate union with the priest, we are about, in his person, to go up the steps of this altar and approach the God who is our only hope and our salvation.

To take part in the Mass is to rise above the world by renouncing Satan, the company of the wicked, and sin; and to unite ourselves with God through Jesus Christ, through His saints, and through the practice of virtue. To take part in the Mass, is then, to be delivered from the evil which saddens us, and to possess the true Good, which is the cause of the true and only Christian joy.

2. CONFITEOR.

See illustration, p. 20.

The priest precedes the *Confiteor* by a versicle from Ps. 123, signing himself.

V/ *Our help is in the name of the Lord* (who is almighty, for it is He...)

R/ *Who made heaven and earth (top picture : a Psalmist).*

In order to approach God, we must be very pure. For this reason, the Church has instituted a sacramental which helps us to acquire a greater purity of heart when we use it. This is the *Confiteor*, in which we accuse ourselves of our faults and incite ourselves to contrition and the love of God, which obtain pardon for us and wipe away our sins. This is for venial sins which do not need the Sacrament of Penance.

The Confession is made to God, before Whom we bow low *(top picture and altar)* for it is His Divine Majesty which we have offended by sin.

This Confession is also made *(top picture)* to Mary, to the Angels *(St. Michael, their head)*, to the Saints *(St. John Baptist, and all the Saints)* and to the Church *(to you, Father, to you, my brethren)*. Our faults offend all those who, as children of God, have His interests at heart ; and they have a harmful repercussion on the whole of the Mystical Body of Christ, of which we impede, each of us, the perfect development.

The Mass is essentially a catholic act, and it tends, as does the whole work of the Redemption, to draw closer the bonds which unite all those who form part of the Communion of the Saints and who are the living members of the Church and of Jesus Christ. It is then to foster the common good of this great living organism that we are acting at the altar, and this explains why the *Confiteor* is a public Confession addressed at the same time to the Church in heaven and to the Church on earth for the accusation of our faults and for the mutual and fraternal help for which we beg. This collective action is a great stimulant and a powerful support. The faithful say the *Confiteor* after the priest.

CONFITEOR: *(Top)* The Psalmist, author of Ps. 123, of which the Church recites a versicle as a prelude to the *Confiteor*, thanks God for having delivered His people. — The Saints, Mary, John the Baptist, Peter and Paul, mention of whom is made in the *Confiteor*. — *(Altar and inset)* The priests bows low as he says the *Confiteor* and strikes his breast at the *mea culpa*. — It is through the Blood of Jesus (Crucifix) that we are forgiven and that Mary obtained the privilege of her Immaculate Conception.

To God :	**Confiteor**... *I confess to almighty God,*
To the Saints :	*to blessed Mary ever Virgin, to blessed Michael the Archangel, to blessed John the Baptist, to the holy Apostles Peter and Paul, to all the Saints,*
To the Church:	*and to you, my brethren (and to you, Father) that I have sinned exceedingly in thought, word, and deed,* *through my fault, through my fault, through my most grievous fault.*

We strike our breasts to show that we wish in a sense to break this heart which has committed sin *(inset)*. This gesture shows, and helps to produce contrition (a word derived from conterere : to break). We do it three times and say with compunction : *mea culpa*. This triple repetition corresponds to sins committed by thought, word, and deed, and it denotes a superlative : a great, a greater, a very great sorrow.

Then we go in inverse order, by asking the Saints and the Church to be our advocates before God, Who alone can wipe away sin.

To the Saints :	*Therefore I beseech blessed Mary ever Virgin, blessed Michael the Archangel, blessed John the Baptist, the holy Apostles Peter and Paul, all the Saints,*
To the Church:	*and you, my brethren (and you, Father)*
To God :	*to pray to the Lord our God for me.*

The priest prays for us, and makes a cross *(inset)*, for everything comes from Calvary.

Prayer :	*May almighty God have mercy upon you, forgive you your sins, and bring you to life everlasting. Amen.*
Absolution :	*May the almighty and merciful Lord grant us pardon, absolution, and remission of our sins. Amen.*

Let us piously make the sign of the Cross to show that it is by virtue of the Passion of our Lord that we obtain the forgiveness for which we have asked *(inset)*.

GOING UP TO THE ALTAR : *(Top)* At the consecration of an altar, the Bishop seals with cement, which has been blessed, the stone of the little grave which has been hollowed out in it, and in which he has placed 3 relics of Saints, of which at least one of a martyr. « It is just », says St. Augustine, « that the martyrs immolated for Jesus Christ should be under the altar on which J.-C. is immolated ; they are there to ask that grace or justice shall triumph over persecutors » (Perist. Hymn V. 515). — *(Altar and inset)* The priest kisses the altar which contains the relics.

3. GOING UP TO THE ALTAR.

Before going up to the altar, the celebrant recites three verses from Ps. 84 and 101. They are expressions of great confidence in God.

V/ *Thou wilt turn, O God, and bring us to life.* R/ *And Thy people shall rejoice in Thee.*

V/ *Show us, O Lord, Thy mercy.* R/ *And grant us Thy salvation.*

V/ *Hear, O Lord, my prayer.* R/ *And let my cry come unto Thee.*

Then comes the ancient salutation of the Hebrews: *Dominus vobiscum* (Ruth II, 4) which has been adopted by the Apostles, and especially by the Liturgy.

V/ *The Lord be with you.* R/ *And with thy spirit.*

Then the priest unclasping his hands, asks the faithful to pray, saying: *Oremus*, and he goes up to the altar reciting a prayer from the Leonian Sacramentary (Vth cent.):

Aufer a nobis...*Take away from us, we beseech Thee, O Lord, our iniquities, that we may be worthy to enter with pure minds into the holy of holies. Through Christ our Lord. Amen.*

The Christian altar deserves the title of Holy of Holies even more fully than the mysterious precincts of the Tabernacle of Moses or of Jerusalem, where God gave out His commands on the *propitiatorium* (mercy seat) between the two Cherubim (described in Isaias VI). Actually the altar perpetuates in our midst the table of Maundy Thursday and the Cross of Good Friday, for at every Mass the atoning Victim of Golgotha is really offered to God and given as food to souls as in the Upper Room.

The altar is also the Holy of Holies, because Christ, Whose Body is now glorified, is at the same time in the Host and the Chalice and in Heaven, which is the real Holy of Holies.

The altar is also the Holy of Holies, because the great miracle of the consecration infallibly ensures for us the presence of the

Son of God, inseparable from the Father and the Holy Ghost. The altar is then truly the *Tabernaculum Dei cum hominibus*.

This is one of the reasons why the priest approaches it and kisses it with love and reverence *(picture of altar)*; but there is another, and that is, that the altar contains the relics of Saints, as he says in the prayer which accompanies this act:

Oramus te, Domine... *We beseech Thee, O Lord, by the merits of Thy Saints, whose relics are here,* (he kisses the altar, see inset) *and of all the Saints, that Thou wouldst vouchsafe to forgive me all my sins. Amen.*

This prayer, like the foregoing one, asks for purity of heart, but this time trusting, as in the *Confiteor* and often during the rest of the Mass, in the merits of the Saints, for they are God's friends, and He hears them willingly. The priest specially invokes the Saints whose precious relics were placed in the altar at the time of its consecration by the Bishop *(top picture)*.

« May the Saints always help us by their powerful merits » said the Bishop as he sealed the stone in which their relics are enclosed. And before this ceremony, the choir had sung this antiphon: « Now you are going to dwell under the altar of God, Saints of God; there, intercede for us with our Lord Jesus Christ ». This is an obvious allusion to the passage in the Apocalypse where St. John says: « I saw under the altar the souls of them that were slain for the word of God and for the testimony which they held » (Apoc. VI, 9). In it he is referring to the martyrs who shed their blood to defend the Gospel, and whose death was a sacrifice associated with the great Martyr on Golgotha. They are also shown near the altar of heaven, which is Christ Himself.

There the High Priest, Jesus, is in glory; here He is hidden in the Host: there the Martyrs are near the altar, which is Christ; here we have their bodies in the altar, which is a symbol of our Lord. The worship given to God in our churches is then identified with that which Christ and the elect give Him in the courts of heaven.

2. PRAYERS AND READINGS.

THE ORDER OF THE MASS IN THE 2nd CENTURY.

Before continuing this explanation of the Mass, we must, in order to understand clearly all that is to follow, remember the way in which the Christian assemblies were conducted, during the first centuries of the Church.

For that it will suffice to quote the great apologist and martyr of the 2nd century, St Justin. He makes a very clear explanation of the Sunday Mass in his *First Apologia* addressed to Antoninus the Pious (138-161). This primitive order has remained essentially the same for 19 centuries as is shown in the present order (pp. 14 and 15).

« *a. On the day, called after the Sun (Sunday), all those living in towns or in the country assemble in the same place.*

b. As long as time allows the memoirs of the Apostles and the writings of the prophets are read. (Reading of the Holy Scriptures: Epistle, Gospel).

c. When the reader has finished, the one who presides speaks to instruct and exhort the people to follow this beautiful teaching. (Homily, Sermon, Preaching).

d. We all rise and pray aloud together. (The Prayers now said only on Good Friday).

e. At the end of the prayers, bread is brought with some wine and water; the one who presides sends up his prayer and thanksgiving to Heaven as earnestly as he can and the people reply by the acclamation: Amen. (Offertory, Consecration).

f. Then takes place the distribution and sharing of the Eucharistic particles. Each one has his share, and the absent ones have theirs sent to them through the ministry of the deacons. (Communion).

g. Those who have plenty, and wish to give, give freely whatever they choose to, and what is collected is given to the one presiding and goes to help orphans, widows, the sick, the poor,

INTROIT : *(Top)* In the VIIIth Century at the Lateran, a Pontifical cortège formed by acolytes bearing candles, 7 subdeacons, 7 deacons, the archdeacon, and the Pope go to the altar while the processional Psalm of entry *(Introitus)* is sung, taken from the Psalms of David. — *(Altar and inset)* The priest says the *Introit* on the Epistle side. He crosses himself as he begins. In Masses for the Dead, this blessing is passed on to them, by the priest making the cross on the Missal.

the prisoners, guests from other communities, in short, all who are in need. (Collection, upkeep of the clergy, almsgiving).

h. *We all assemble on the day of the Sun, because it is the first day when God, making matter from the darkness, created the world, and because this same day our Saviour Jesus Christ rose from the dead ».* (The Christian Sunday instead of the Jewish Sabbath).

It is the official putting into action every Sunday of the *Magisterial* and *Ministerial* powers that Christ gave his Church when He charged Her to continue His *Mission of teaching and sanctifying* through the centuries. And we again find here our two great divisions of the Mass, that of the *Catechumens* and that of the *Faithful* (p. 13 below).

4. INTROIT.

The prayers which the priest said at the foot of the altar (pp. 16-24) are preparatory prayers, which make up the first part of the « Mass of the Catechumens ».

The 2nd part begins with the *Introit* which is, as its name shows, an entrance song, originally designed to occupy the faithful whilst the Pontiff and his procession were leaving the sacristy and going into the sanctuary *(top picture)*.

This song was introduced into the Roman liturgy in the VIth century. Nowadays the choir sings it in the sung Masses whilst the priest goes to the foot of the altar and says there with his assistants the *Judica* and *Confiteor*. It is only after going up to the altar, and during the singing of the *Kyrie*, that the celebrant reads the *Introit* : this custom comes from Low Mass where the priest says it then whilst making the sign of the Cross *(altar and inset)*.

The *Introit* is a Psalm, with an antiphon taken mostly from the psalm itself. This antiphon was repeated as a refrain after each versicle until the priest arrived at the altar. Now only the antiphon remains, one psalm-verse, the Gloria and again the antiphon.

The *Introit* is the first element of the Mass which varies with the calendar. Thus it inculcates in the faithful the spirit of the feast which is celebrated.

KYRIE: *(Top)* The blind man of Jericho, the Canaanite woman, the ten lepers, go with confidence to Jesus crying to Him this short but expressive, this touching but forceful supplication: « Have mercy on us ». — *(Altar and inset)* The celebrant in the centre of the altar, joins his hands and says alternately with the server (and if possible with the people) three times *Kyrie Eleison* to God the Father, *Christe Eleison* to God the Son, and *Kyrie Eleison* to God the Holy Ghost.

5. KYRIE ELEISON.

The *Introit* is followed by a litany (this word in Greek means supplication) which the priest says alternately with the server or the people at low Mass. It is the *Kyrie*; also it is found at the beginning and end of the *Litanies of the Saints*. On Holy Saturday and on the vigil of Pentecost the *Litanies* are sung, and their last *Kyrie* is the *Kyrie* of the Mass.

Kyrie Eleison. These two Greek words mean : *Lord have mercy on us*, which would be translated in Latin : *Domine, miserere*.

This exclamation is often found in Holy Scripture. In the Old Testament, David uses it (Ps. IV, 2 ; VI, 3 ; IX, 14 ; XXV, 11 ; L. 3), Isaias (XXXIII, 2), Tobias (VIII, 10), etc., etc.

The Gospel in its turn shows that it was in popular use :

By the road to Jericho where Jesus was passing, Bartimeus the blind man cried : *Jesus, Son of David, have mercy on me*. And as they tried to silence him, threatening him, he cried out the more : *Son of David, have mercy on me*. Jesus said to him : *Go, thy faith hath made thee whole (top picture)*. And straightway he received his sight (Cf. Mark. X, 46-52).

Jesus being in the neighbourhood of Tyre and Sidon, a Canaanite woman approached Him *(top picture)* and cried out, saying : *Have mercy on me, Lord, Son of David* ; my daughter is grievously tormented by a devil... O woman, answered Jesus, great is thy faith : be it done to thee even as thou wilt. And her daughter was healed (Cf. Matt. XV, 21-28).

As Jesus was entering a village, there met Him ten men who were lepers ; who stood afar off and they lifted up their voices *(top picture)* saying : *Jesus, Master, have mercy on us*. He said to them : Go, show yourselves to the priests. And as they went they were healed (Cf. Luke XVII, 12-14).

The Church at Antioch was the first to use this formula, as the response of the people to the prayers which the Deacon addressed to God : as litanies to precede the Mass of the Catechumens.

These prayers of litany soon spread from this centre throughout the East, notably to Jerusalem and Byzantium and later penetrated to Rome, Milan and throughout the West. The 2nd Council of Vaison held by St Cesarius of Arles in 529, says: « Since the good and salutary custom has been introduced in Rome as well as in all the provinces of Italy and the East, of often repeating the *Kyrie Eleison* with great devotion and compunction, we order that this pious practice be introduced also during Mass in all our churches » (Mansi VIII).

Here is a portion of the requests in form of litany and kept in the Byzantine liturgy:

THE DEACON: To obtain peace from on high and salvation for our souls, let us pray to the Lord. — CHOIR: *Kyrie Eleison*.

THE DEACON: For our Bishop, for the venerable sacerdotal order, for the deacons of Christ and for the people, let us pray to the Lord. — CHOIR: *Kyrie Eleison*.

THE DEACON: For this holy place of abode, for the whole city, for this country and for the faithful living in it. — CHOIR: *Kyrie Eleison*.

Saint Gregory, Pope at the end of the VIth century, explains that in Rome, where the *Kyrie* was introduced at the beginning of that same century, they suppressed the requests « at the daily Masses so that we can spend more time and attention on the words of supplication *Kyrie Eleison* » (Lett. IX to John of Syracuse). This became usual. He also adds that in Rome is said: *Christe Eleison*, which was not done by the Greeks.

The number of the invocations was fixed at nine to make of them a trinitarian prayer:

God the Father. — *Lord have mercy* (3 times alternately).

God the Son. — *Christ have mercy* (3 times alternately).

God the Holy Ghost. — *Lord have mercy* (3 times alternately).

6. GLORIA IN EXCELSIS.
See illustration, p. 32.

On days when the *Te Deum* has been said at Matins, the priest says the *Gloria*, which is a hymn of praise to God, taken from the Byzantine liturgy as was the *Kyrie*.

St Paul wrote to the Ephesians : « Be filled with the Holy Spirit, speaking to one another in psalms and hymns and spiritual canticles, singing and making melody in your hearts to the Lord » (V. 18-19).

And Fortescue draws attention to the fact that « the Christians of the first centuries began to compose texts to be sung, on the model of the only hymn-book they knew, the Psalter. These private psalms (as opposed to the canonical psalms) were written in short verses like the Psalter. Such are the *Te Deum*, the so-called Athanasian Creed, best known and certainly finest of all, the *Gloria in excelsis* » (The Mass, p. 239).

In the collection of the *Apostolic Constitutions* (VII, 47), end of the 4th century, this hymn is addressed to the Father: «We adore Thee through Thy High Priest... because of Thy great glory... Lord God, Father of Christ the Lamb of God who takest away the sins of the world, receive our prayers, Thou who sittest above the Cherubim, for Thou alone art holy, etc... ».

After the Councils of Nicaea (325) and of Constantinople (381) which affirmed against the heretics the divinity of Jesus and of the Holy Ghost, this hymn was rearranged and it became the great Trinitarian doxology. After the Father, Christ is addressed as one who shares with the Holy Ghist the glory of the Father. In fact, the phrase « *sedes ad dexteram Patris* » means that the humanity of Jesus is united to the divinity of the Person of the Word since the Incarnation and is glorified in Heaven since the Ascension.

It was under this new form that Rome introduced the *Gloria* into the Mass ; and it was used originally at the first Mass of Christmas, as this hymn is the paraphrase made by the Church of the Angels' hymn at the birth of Jesus *(top picture)*.

Glory to God   *Glory be to God in the highest,*

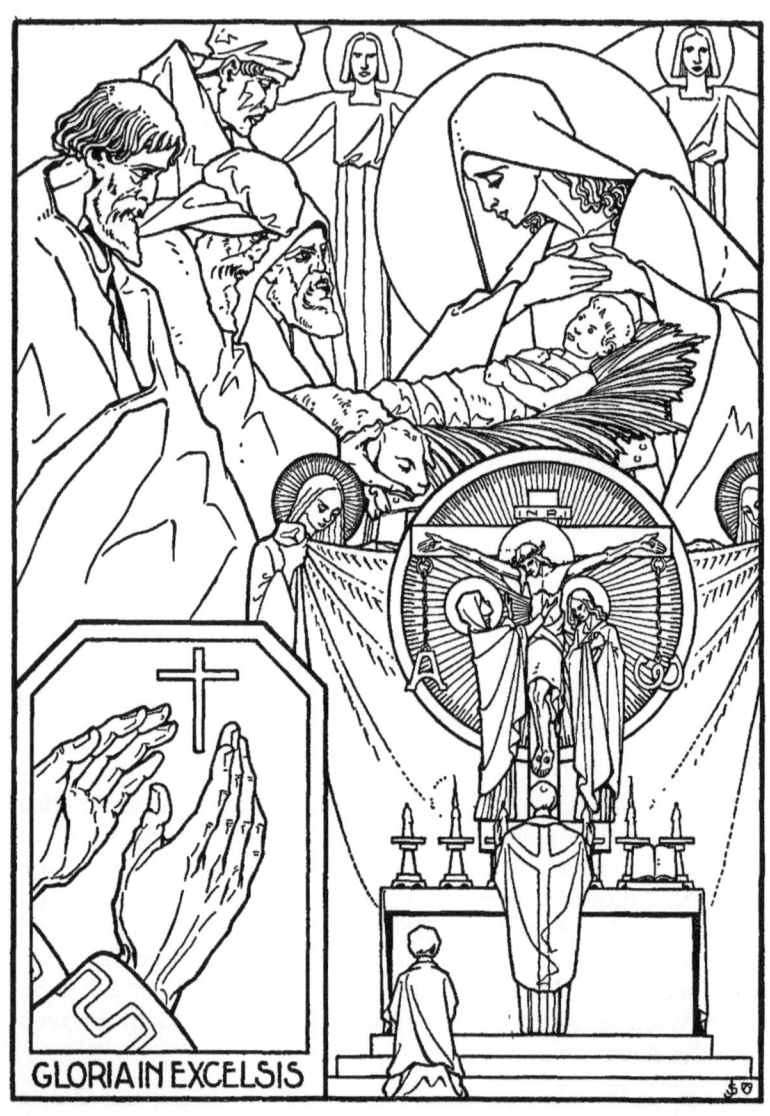

GLORIA IN EXCELSIS: *(Top)* « An angel of the Lord appeared to the shepherds and said to them: I bring you tidings of great joy which shall be to all the people, for there is born to you a Saviour Who is Christ the Lord. And immediately there were with the angel a multitude of the heavenly host, praising God and saying: Glory be to God on high and peace on earth to men of good will » (Luke II, 9-14). — *(Altar and inset)* The priest extends his hands whilst intoning the *Gloria*.

And on earth peace to men of good will.

1) Father *We praise Thee, we bless Thee.*
We adore Thee, we glorify Thee.
We give Thee thanks for Thy great glory.

Lord God, heavenly King, God the Father almighty.

2) Son *Lord Jesus Christ, the only begotten Son,*

Lord God, Lamb of God, Son of the Father,

Thou Who takest away the sins of the world, have mercy on us.

Thou Who takest away the sins of the world, receive our prayer.

Thou Who sittest at the right hand of the Father, have mercy on us.

For Thou alone art holy, Thou alone art the Lord, Thou alone art most high, Jesus Christ.

3) Holy Ghost : *With the Holy Ghost, in the glory of God the Father. Amen.*

The glory of the God of Heaven is assured since the Messianic peace has come on earth in the person of Jesus and through Him it pervades men of good will, that is to say, those who wish for this glory and peace. Glory is defined « *notitia cum laude* ». God is glorified in the measure that He is known and that this knowledge is expressed by praise. This praise comes from this knowledge and it is increased in us and in those who hear the divine greatness proclaimed. The object of this knowledge and adoring praise is the omnipotence which the Father shows in the fulfilling of the mysteries of the Redemption. This object of our adoration is thus the Lamb of God, Who takes away the sins of the world and Who hearkens all the more to our prayers, since He reigns in glory in Heaven with the Father and the Holy Ghost.

COLLECT: *(Top)* Jesus shows His glorious wounds to His Father so that the merits of Calvary may be applied to our souls. — *(Altar and inset)* After kissing the altar, symbol of Christ, the priest says the Collect: hands slightly outstretched in imitation of the position of Jesus on the Cross *(De Orat. XIV)*. And he ends: « *Per Dominum nostrum Jesum Christum. Through Jesus Christ our Lord.* »

7. COLLECT.

Christian prayer said together at the altar has three forms: the prayer of *litany* which is the *Kyrie*, the *collective* prayer which is the *Collect*, the *Secret* and the *Postcommunion* and the *Eucharistic* prayer during which the Consecration takes place.

The **Collect** which follows the *Kyrie* or *Gloria* is called *Oratio ad collectam*, because it was said by the gathering assembled in a church in Rome, whence a procession moved towards another church where the Station was held and Mass celebrated. This prayer *ad collectam* was, as a general rule, repeated on arrival at this second church, and so became the collective prayer called *Collect*.

Thus the Roman Rite starts the Mass of the Catechumens, as is done by the liturgy of Constantinople, by a litany and hymn followed by a prayer.

Before the Collect the celebrant addresses to the people what might be called the Christian greeting : V/ **Dominus vobiscum :** *The Lord be with you.* — R/ *Et cum spiritu tuo : And with thy spirit.*

Then the celebrant calls the assembly to prayer : *Oremus*. At certain days the deacon told the people to kneel : *Flectamus genua*, as is still done on Good Friday, the Ember days, etc. And the assembly prayed in silence until the moment when the *Levate* was sung. The celebrant then gathered up the wishes of all the assembly in one prayer which was in very truth the « collection », the collect from all hearts. This is the second reason why the name is given to this prayer. In fact, at all Masses, the *Collect* unites the feelings of all the assembly, and the priest says it aloud so as to fuse all the requests into one which is that of the Church.

The prayer of litany, then much longer, was directed by the deacon ; it was the part of the priest to say the *collective* and the *Eucharistic prayers*. The faithful participate in these three prayers by the responses : *Amen*.

The *Collects* are thus sacerdotal prayers. The greater number of them are found in the Sacramentaries of popes St Leo, St Gelasius and St Gregory (6th to 8th century), which were the books used by the priest at the altar in those days. Alluding to these books pope Celestine V said : These sacerdotal observances are uniformly celebrated throughout the Catholic Church, so that the rule of prayer becomes the rule of faith : « *legem credendi lex statuat supplicandi* » *(Epist. ad Episc. Galliarum, cap. 11)*.

These very ancient prayers are indeed one of the channels of Christian tradition. Their harmonious rhythm called *cursus*, their simplicity, vigour, exactness and variety ensure to their dogmatic and moral dynamism a penetration which resembles that of the inspired Psalms and Canticles.

What gives to the *Collects* an unequalled value, is that they are the *official* prayer of the Church, that is to say, the prayer through which all the hierarchy : the Pope, the Bishops and in their name all the priests, speak to God in as much as they are the authentic representatives of Christ, Who is our only Mediator with God in Heaven *(top picture)*.

This prayer is an exterior one because it comes from a visible society, but it is none the less a more intensely interior prayer than any other. It is, in the fullest sense, the prayer of the Mystical Body of Christ : Head and members. As a prayer which is one, holy, Roman, Catholic and Apostolic, it is made by the Church on earth in entire dependence on the « High Priest Who possesses an eternal priesthood (Who has therefore neither substitute nor successor) and Who can save all those who approach God through Him, living always to intercede in our favour » (Hebr. VII, 24-25). « If you ask the Father anything in my name he will give it to you » (John XVI, 23) so declared Jesus at the Last Supper. And the apostolic Church obeying this command addresses her Collects to God the Father « *Per Dominum nostrum Jesum Christum* ».

In replying : *Amen*, all the faithful mark as with a seal or signature this petition addressed to God on their behalf by the Church and through Jesus.

8. EPISTLE.
See illustration, p. 38.

The Collect is followed by the **Epistle** : this recalls the description of St Justin (p. 25) which showed the Sunday Mass of the 2nd Century in Rome beginning with readings from the *Memoirs of the Apostles* and the *Prophets*.

In this description there are no prayers before the Homily (p. 25 *d*) and this Apologist gives the reason for it : « We say the prayer (as is still said on Good Friday), after we have heard the truth, to show that we are people leading a good life and faithful to the precepts received for our eternal salvation » (Apol. LXV, 1). The readings and the preaching reminded the Christians of their obligations. They then asked God for the grace to enable them to put these into practice.

But the Church allowed these prayers to fall into disuse, either because in the 5th century similar supplications were introduced in the Eucharistic prayer (the *Te igitur* for example, p. 73), or because the Collect introduced later had replaced them.

In the reunions which they held every Sabbath day in their Synagogues, the Jews read their Scriptures, i. e. the Old Testament distributed on a period of three years.

The Sabbath was the day which commemorated the Lord's rest after the Creation and which represented the eternal beatitude, consisting essentially in the vision of God. The Jews prepared in some measure for this happiness during the day of rest, by contemplating and meditating on the divine truths contained in the Scriptures, revealed by the Spirit of God to Moses and to the prophets of Israel. Like us, the just of the Old Law were saved by their faith in one God and in Jesus Whom He was to send as Redeemer ; and this faith was fostered in them specially by the reading of the Mosaic Law and by prophecies concerning Christ and His Kingdom.

The first Christians, in their Sunday reunions did what the Jews had done in their Sabbath reunions ; but to the reading of the Old Testament they added that of the New. « The Church of Rome, says Tertullian, joins to the Laws and the Prophets, the

EPISTLE: *(Top)* St Paul imprisoned in Rome writes one of his 14 immortal letters, which were read during his lifetime in the first Christian communities and which are still read in all the churches of the world. He is supremely the « Apostle of Jesus Christ » to the Gentiles, that is to say, our Apostle. — *(Altar and inset)* The priest begins the *Epistle* by saying: Reading from the Acts of the Apostles or from Epistle of the Blessed Apostle Peter (Paul, John, James, Jude). At the end the response is: *Deo gratias*.

writings of the Apostles and the Evangelists, so as to nourish the faith » *(De Praescript.).* In Milan at the time of St Ambrose, the lessons of the Mass were three in number, a reading of the *Prophets* (Old Testament), a reading of the *Apostles* (Epistle), a reading of the *Gospel* (Gospel). St Augustine similarly indicates « the Prophet, the Apostle and the Gospel » (In Ps. 118).

Gradually the reading of the Prophets fell into disuse and only the Epistle and Gospel were left; but under the title Epistle, passages are sometimes read from the Old Testament.

The arrangement of the Epistles in the Roman Missal dates back to a period at the time of St Gregory († 604). At Easter and Christmas, at Ascension and Pentecost, during Lent, and during Advent they have been chosen to conform with the object or the spirit of these feasts and liturgical seasons. For the rest of the temporal Cycle the principle of the *Lectio continua*, adopted for the Breviary, has been applied. From Low Sunday to Pentecost and after Pentecost to the feast of SS. Peter and Paul, the catholic Epistles are read. Then come the « Pauline Epistles », in the Vulgate order, to the Romans, Corinthians, Galatians, Ephesians, Philippians, Colossians, which are continued after the Epiphany. For the Saints, passages have been taken from the Old or New Testament which glorify the virtues which they practised.

These readings allow us to quench our thirst at the very source of divine life. Anxious to sanctify our souls, for which she is responsible, the Church bids us listen to the very word of God, for in listening to the reading of the Epistles we learn from the mouth of Moses, the Prophets and the Apostles, the supernatural truths which the Holy Ghost and the Son of God have revealed to them. « Moses, the Prophets, the Apostles and the Evangelists, says St Cyril of Alexandria, are sources of salvation to us, for they communicate to us the word of God » *(Contra Julian, 1, VIII).*

MUNDA COR: *(Top)* An angel takes a burning coal and symbolically cleanses the lips of Isaias: this symbolizes that so purified he is fitted to announce the Prophecies of the Lord. — *(Altar and inset)* The priest bows profoundly and says the *Munda cor* while the server carries the Missal over to the Gospel side. In union with the priest let us pray for our souls to be cleansed that the light of the Gospel may enter therein. Then we stand and listen with respect to the word of God.

9. GRADUAL — ALLELUIA — TRACT.

The Jews in their Synagogue service separated the reading from the Law and that from the Prophets by a chant made up of the *Psalms*. The Church has done the same, and has inserted the **Gradual** (the Psalms sung on the *steps* of the ambo) between the Epistle and the Gospel. The *Gradual* is made up of two separate Psalms, of which the first is the real *Gradual* and this was said after the reading from the Prophets, which has since disappeared from the Mass. The second is called the **Alleluia** because it is preceded by that Hebrew acclamation « Praise the Lord » which was sung in the Synagogues, and which St. John heard sung in Heaven (Apoc. XIX, 1). The *Gradual* as it is at present has retained only two verses of the Psalm and the *Alleluia* one. When at certain seasons of the year the *Alleluia* is omitted its place is taken by another chant called the **Tract**. This is a Psalm, reduced nowadays to a few verses.

The Psalms, alternating with the readings, help the doctrine by song and prayer to impress the minds of the faithful. God speaks to His people, who hear Him in silence ; then the people, enlightened and inspired by the divine truth, speak to God : « How swiftly, writes St. Augustine, did the Psalms lead me to Thee, and with what fire did they consume me » (Conf. 4). « The Psalms, says the pseudo-Denis, include *by way of praise* all that is contained in Holy Scripture » (Hier. eccl. C. 3).

The Psalter is of the utmost importance because it is part of the inspired Canon of Holy Writ. « David was the harp of the Holy Ghost » said Hesychius of Jerusalem (Quaest. 28). « Asaph composed his Psalms under the inspiration of the Holy Ghost » said Eusebius of Cesarea *(Dem. ev. LX)*. « The Psalms were composed under the inspiration of the Holy Ghost and they are His » says St. Ephrem (Necros. can. 7).

The Psalms, like the whole of the Old Testament, foretell the New Covenant. By singing them Israel expressed both the figure and the reality. « All things must needs be fulfilled which are written in the law of Moses and in the prophets and in the psalms, concerning me », explained Christ. (*Luke XXIV*, 44).

Christ sang all of the Psalms in the synagogue ; the Apostles did the same and St. Paul wrote to the Ephesians: Speak together in Psalms. Throughout the world priests recite the Psalms each morning at Mass, and during the day in their Breviary. Thus they too express both the figure and the reality of the mystery of the Kingdom of Heaven, for the Church militant is at one and the same time the prelude to, and the figure of the Kingdom which is to come. Which gives us an excellent reason why the Holy Ghost, animating principle of the Mystical Body of Christ, has inspired the Psalms to serve as the prayers of its Head and members. « The voice of him who speaks in the Psalms is universal, says St. Augustine. His head is in Heaven. But his voice ? — the voice which in the Psalms sings, in sorrowful sighs or is full of joy ? That voice we should recognize as our own. If each of us remains in the Body of Christ, He will speak through us... His voice is ours and ours is His » *(In Ps. 62)*.

10. MUNDA COR.
See illustration, p. 40.

Isaias saw in a vision the Son of God in all the splendour of His majesty, before Whom the Seraphim sang their *Sanctus* (p. 69). The Prophet, overcome by the sight of this glory, realized that he was too lowly and unclean to be the spokesman of so great a God. But an angel purified him with a burning coal taken from the altar *(top picture)*, and thenceforward Isaias was fitted to speak as a Prophet before the people of God.

The priest, immediately before he reads aloud the Gospel, which is the very word of the Son of God and the radiation of His glory, is conscious of this same unworthiness and prays to God :

Munda cor... *Cleanse my heart and my lips, O almighty God, Who didst cleanse the lips of the prophet Isaias with a burning coal: vouchsafe through Thy gracious mercy so to cleanse me that I may worthily proclaim Thy holy Gospel. Through Christ our Lord. Amen* (inset).

11. GOSPEL.
See illustration, p. 44.

The **Gospel** is the climax of the Mass of the Catechumens because it is the revelation of the mysteries of the Kingdom of God in all its clarity. For it is no longer the writings of a *Prophet* or an *Apostle* which are read; it is the *Son of God* Himself, He Who inspired and taught them, Who speaks to us.

« *God*, says St. Paul, *who at sundry times* (a piece at a time) *and in divers manners* (dreams, visions, etc.) *spoke in times past to the Fathers* (the Patriarchs, Moses, etc.) *by the Prophets* (David, etc.), *last of all, in these days, hath* (Messianic age) *spoken to us by his Son* (the Incarnate Word) *who is the brightness of his glory* » (Hebr. I, 1-3).

From all eternity the Father says to Himself, by His mental word which is *the Word*, all that He is in Himself and all that He can create *ad extra*. This Word, spiritually begotten by the Father, is the Son of God or the infinite thought by which God knows Himself adequately. This Word became flesh and throughout the whole of His life, by His example, by His preaching and by His miracles, He reveals to us the divine secrets which the Father makes known to Him by His eternal generation, and which His human soul has contemplated in the Beatific Vision from the first moment of its creation.

The Gospel is filled with proof of this: « I speak of that which the Father has taught me... If you remain in my word, you shall know the truth, and the truth will make you free... He who is of God hears the word of God. You do not hear because you are not of God... While you have the light with you, believe in the light, that you may be the children of light... I do not call you my servants but my friends, because all that I have learnt from my Father I have taught unto you... Father, glorify Thy Son that Thy Son also may glorify Thee by giving eternal life to all those Thou hast confided to him. But eternal life, it is that they should know Thee, the only true God, and him whom Thou hast sent: Jesus Christ » (St. John passim).

The Church reads the Gospel, which tells of the life and teaching of Christ, so as to communicate to us that eternal life

GOSPEL: *(Top)* Jesus preaches. — *(Altar and inset)* The priest says *Dominus vobiscum* and *Sequentia* . *Continuation of the holy Gospel according to St. Matthew* etc. and makes the sign of the Cross on the book, then on his forehead, lips and breast. He does this that the word of life may enter into his mind and heart, and that it may be expressed in his speech. The response is: *Gloria*, Glory be to Thee, O Lord. At the end of the Gospel the priest kisses the book with respect, saying: *By the words of the Gospel may our sins be blotted out.* Faith and love strengthened by this holy reading will wipe away our venial faults.

which He possesses as God and in the plenitude of which he partakes as Man. Later she gives to us the Eucharist which is Jesus Christ Himself. By these two means the Church develops in our souls a faith and love which makes us adhere more and more closely to Him Who, in Heaven and in the Host, sees God face to face and Who has said : « No one knoweth the Father but the Son, and he to whom it shall please the Son to reveal Him » (Matt. XI, 27).

« Do not lose a single word of the Gospel, says Origen ; because if, when you are receiving Holy Communion, you rightly take care to see that not even the smallest particle falls, why should you not believe that it is wrong to neglect even a single word of Jesus Christ » (Hom. XIII, In exod. sanctis myst.).

When we listen to the Gospel expressing the divine thoughts of Christ there is a spiritual link between us and Him, and we become like the children of the family round the table of their Lord, eating « *the bread of life* » (John. VI, 35). Thus do we prepare ourselves to receive the Eucharistic bread in Which the divine life is given to us in even greater abundance. All this explains why nothing is more precious, nothing to be more reverenced, after the most holy Sacrament of the altar, than the « *verbum vitae* » contained in the Gospel.

As was the case for the Epistles, the Church chooses the Gospels to correspond with the great feasts, with the liturgical seasons and with the feast of each Saint. For the rest, the Gospel of St. John is read from Easter to Pentecost, the beginning of St. Matthew, of St. Mark and St. Luke from the Epiphany to Septuagesima, and the end of these same Synoptic Gospels from Pentecost to Advent.

The Epistles end with the response *Deo Gratias* and the Gospels with the cry of admiration and praise : *Laus tibi Christe, Praise be to Thee, O Christ !*

CREDO: *(Top)* An Ecumenical Council. The Bishops are grouped around the Pope, the Vicar of Christ, and form with him the unique Magisterium of the universal Church. They explain, with an infallibility which the Holy Spirit assures to them, the true meaning of the Scriptures and in particular of the Gospels, which lie open on a throne in the midst of them. — *(Altar and inset)* The priest intones the Credo, raising and extending his hands; he genuflects at: *Incarnatus est*, and makes the sign of the Cross at the end.

12. CREDO.

After the *Epistle* the Church sang *Psalms* : after the Gospel she sings the *Credo*, which is a development of the Apostles Creed. This is once again the *notitia cum laude* or the praise of Him Who has revealed to us His transcendence (v. p. 31 and 42).

« No prophecy of scripture », says the Prince of the Apostles, « is made by private interpretation » (II Pet. 1, 20). Holy Writ, which contains the word of God, must be explained by the Church, for the Holy Spirit assures to her alone an infallible Magisterium to do this. This universal Church exercises this Magisterium particularly by Ecumenical Councils. So at Mass, which is one of the forms of her ordinary Magisterium, the Church directs that the Credo shall be read. Herein the Councils of Nicaea (325) and of Constantinople (381) have expressed in phrases, which come either from Scripture or from other documents provided by written or oral Traditoin, the mystery of the Blessed Trinity and of the salvation of men by the Word Incarnate and by His Church.

(The part in italics is that which was made by the Council of Nicaea).

Credo *in unum DEUM* ... I believe in one God.

PATREM — *the Father almighty, Creator of Heaven and earth, of all things visible and invisible.*

FILIUM — And in one Lord, Jesus Christ, the only-begotten Son of God, born of the Father before all ages : *God of God, light of light, true God of true God ; begotten, not made, consubstantial with the Father, by Whom all things were made.*

Who for us men, and for our salvation, came down from Heaven, and was incarnate by the Holy Ghost of the Virgin Mary, *and was made man.*

He was crucified also for us under Pontius Pilate, *He suffered,* and was buried. *And the third day He rose again* according to the Scriptures, *and ascended into Heaven ;* He sitteth at the right hand of the Father. *And He shall come again* with glory, *to judge both the living and the dead :* of Whose Kingdom there shall be no end.

SPIRITUM — *And I believe in the Holy Ghost*, the Lord and giver of life, Who proceedeth from the Father [and the Son], Who together with the Father and the Son is adored and glorified, Who spoke by the Prophets.

ECCLESIAM — And in one, holy, Catholic and Apostolic Church.

I confess one baptism for the remission of sins.

And I look for the resurrection of the dead, and the life of the world to come. *Amen*.

Active participation in the Mass of the Catechumens helps the members of the Mystical Body, who so submit themselves to the Magisterium of the Church, to think in unity with their Head and to grow in the knowledge of God which they draw from authentic sources.

It is also the best way of acquiring the dispositions required for active participation in the Eucharistic sacrifice and in Holy Communion which is the practice of the *Ministerial Power* which is exercised principally during the *Mass of the Faithful*.

To participate thus at Mass is to go :

through *Jesus in the Church* (minister of *Christ the King*, the Church presides over liturgical actions),

through *Jesus in the Gospel* (organ of *Christ the Prophet*, the Church preaches His word),

through *Jesus in the Eucharist* (instrument of *Christ the Priest*, the Church offers this sacrifice of love,

to the *Father*, all-powerful, to the *Son*, wisdom of the Father, and to the *Holy Spirit*, Their bond of love !

Such is, in outline, the divine plan which the Scriptures reveal to us, and which consists, for all men of good will, in glorifying the infinite mercy of God by participation through Christ, with Christ and in Christ, in an integral life of light and love.

II. MASS OF THE FAITHFUL

1. PREPARATION OF THE SACRIFICE : *From the Offertory to the Preface.*

13. THE OFFERTORY — 14. SUSCIPE SANCTE PATER : Oblation of the host without stain.
See illustration, p. 50.

The « Mass of the Faithful » or the sacrifice proper begins with the *Offertory* and renews the sacrifice of the Last Supper which foreshadowed the sacrifice of Calvary.

At the Last Supper Jesus took the unleavened bread which was eaten with the Paschal Lamb, into his hands *(top picture)*. At Mass, the priest likewise takes a host made of unleavened wheat flour, and lifting up the paten on which it lies, he contemplates the victim which he is about to immolate *(altar and inset)*; he expresses, in terms and ideas which recur in the Canon of the Mass (p. 73, 83 etc.), the ends for which he offers this sacrifice to God.

Suscipe .. *Receive, O Holy Father, almighty and eternal God, this spotless host, which I, Thy unworthy servant, offer unto Thee, my living and true God, for mine own countless sins, offenses and negligences, and for all here present; as also for all faithful Christians living and dead, that it may avail for my own and their salvation unto life eternal. Amen.*

On the cross the Incarnate Word, the Head of all humanity, offered himself voluntarily in sacrifice to his Father. By this offering, carried out in a spirit of humility, reverence, love and obedience, amid tremendous physical and moral suffering, the Man-God solemnly acknowledged in our name that God is our sovereign Lord (the generic nature of all sacrifice) and reconciled us in complete justice with the Godhead (specific nature of Christ's sacrifice which is propitiatory).

Now whenever the Church offers the Eucharistic sacrifice, Christ himself is made present under the species of bread and wine which for a special reason, in virtue of the twofold consecration, represent the separation of his Blood from his Body

SUSCIPE SANCTE PATER: *(Top)* Jesus at the Last Supper takes unleavened bread, with which was eaten the Paschal Lamb: « Accepit Jesus panem » (Mat. XXVI, 26). — *(Altar)* Having said the *Dominus vobiscum* and the Offertory Antiphon, the priest spreads the corporal on the altar, removes the veil and the pall which cover the chalice, and offers up the host which rests on the paten, saying: *Suscipe*. The small hosts are in a ciborium or on the paten *(inset)*. The server brings the cruets.

effected on Golgotha. In consequence the Mass possesses those properties of adoration, atonement, purification and sanctification which belong to Calvary. But in order to benefit from this offering of the Body and Blood of Jesus, and to cause others to benefit from it, those present must take a certain part. As the one priest and Victim of the sacrifice of the Last Supper and of Calvary, Christ does not offer in his own name alone but as the Head of his mystical body and in the name of this whole body. In the same way the Church renews this sacrificial oblation at the altar in the name of all the faithful, and particularly of those present with the same sentiments of offering which Jesus has. To the offering of the Head should be added, therefore, the offering of the members: at least a *virtual* offering which consists in having that same intention, even if only implicitly, that the Church has when her priests perform this ritual act of the *virtue of religion*. For Christians in a state of grace this offering becomes formal, if by an interior act of the virtue of charity they offer themselves as complementary victims (i.e. which are no essential or integral part of the sacrifice). Thus by their agency Jesus « fills up those things that are wanting » in his Passion (*Col. 1*, 24) and this consists precisely in his members uniting themselves *morally* with the sacrifice of their Head, by dying to sin in order to live ever more fully of his divine life. This is the ultimate aim and the final result of the consecration and communion, rites to which the offertory refers.

At one time, indeed, during the singing of a Psalm, called the *Offertory*, of which now only a verse remains, the faithful brought the bread and wine required for the offering and consumption of the divine Victim. These offerings they set apart from their own possessions which were thus referred to God the author of all things. This practice now no longer exists save in the form of an offering and collection at the Offertory or as the stipend for a Mass. The faithful should be encouraged to place in thought their small host on the paten showing in this way their desire to be closely united to Jesus, Victim on the altar and Bread of life at the holy Table.

DEUS QUI HUMANÆ: *(Top)* Jesus at the Last Supper pours water into the cup of wine. — *(Altar)* After having made the sign of the Cross with the paten on the corporal *(see picture inset p. 50)* in memory of the Passion, the priest places the host on the corporal; then turning to the Epistle side, he wipes the chalice with the purificator and pours wine into it *(inset)*. Saying: *Deus qui humanæ*, etc. he makes the sign of the Cross on the water cruet *(ibid.)* and pours a few drops into the chalice.

15. DEUS QUI HUMANÆ : The fusion of the wine and the water.

At the Last Supper Jesus took the cup of wine called the « chalice of benediction » (Cf. I, Cor. X, 16) because the Jews used to drink it, while thanking God for their deliverance out of Egypt. The wine according to the Jewish ritual used to be mixed with water *(top picture)*. The priest conforming to the words of S. Cyprian *(Ep. 63)* « Our Lord taught us by his example and by his word » pours into the chalice the wine and a few drops of water *(Altar and picture inset)*.

The Church added symbolic meanings to this historical and fundamental one. In the Byzantine Liturgy it is customary to pierce the bread with a « lance » saying : « One of the soldiers with a spear pierced his side, and immediately there came out blood and water ». The Eucharist is thus clearly the sacrament or sign of the Passion.

In the West there is a further symbolic meaning to be added. It is the divinisation of Christians by their union with Jesus in his oblation of purest love.

St Cyprian says : « Because Christ carried us all within Himself in bearing our sins, we may visualise the water as the symbol of Christian people, and the wine, as that of our Lord's blood. Hence, when the Chalice of our Lord is consecrated, it would be unbecoming for it to contain either the wine or the water separately, for if the wine alone was offered Christ would be represented without us, and likewise if the water was offered by itself this would show the faithful without Christ. But when the elements are mixed the spiritual and heavenly mystery is accomplished » *(Ep. 63, 13)*.

In mixing a little water with the wine, the Church joins as it were, the sacrifice of her members to that of her Divine Head. St. Augustine writes : « God shows this mystery (i. e. her oblation with Jesus) to His Church in the daily sacrifice she offers, for, as she is the Body of so great a Head she learns to offer herself up through Him ». *(De Civ. Dei, X, c. 20)*. Christian souls should consider this fact and lead lives of such perfection as to make all their actions worthy offerings to God. They will then be able to say of everything they do : Here is another drop of myself poured into the chalice of all Masses. Under these conditions our life will become worthy of members of Christ's Mystical Body and will grow into a living extension of the mystery of the Incarnation. Thus speaks the Church while joining to this rite a prayer which is a collect of the Leonian Sacramentary for the feast of the Nativity.

Deus qui... *O God who in creating human nature didst wonderfully dignify it and hast still more wonderfully renewed it (mirabilius reformasti), grant that* (this part of the sentence has been added) : « *by the mystery of this water and this wine* » *we may be made partakers of His Divinity who vouchsafed to become partaker of our humanity, Jesus Christ Thy Son our Lord, who being God, liveth and reigneth with Thee in the unity of the Holy Ghost.*

God, who had made Adam a masterpiece of Creation and had endowed him with gifts of divine grace, created a second Adam surpassing him by far, for Christ Who possesses divine nature as the Son of God, also possesses the human nature of His mother Mary. These two natures, are united in the Person of the Word, born of the Father from all eternity. Christ's personal being is Divine and His humanity overflows with the grace of the Holy Spirit. The Son of God made man redeemed us by His precious blood (Cf. *1 Cor. VI, 20*) so that in becoming his members « we partake through Him of the divine nature », as the Church says here with St Peter. *(2 Peter I, 4).*

This mysterious union of which the mixture of the wine and water is a symbol, becomes a living reality in Communion. The « blood of the grape » *(Ecclus. 50, 16)* is changed into the « Blood of Jesus » and flows through the « branches of the mystical Body » producing in them the fruits of divine grace. Such is the allegory which Christ developed at the Last Supper when he said : « I am the Vine; you are the branches » *(John 15, 5) (top picture).*

16. OFFERIMUS TIBI : Oblation of the Chalice of Salvation.
See illustration, p. 56.

The Eucharistic sacrifice does not consist in offering bread and wine to God, but in offering the Body and Blood of Jesus under the appearances of bread and wine. The priest, therefore, lifting up the chalice *(altar and inset)* asks in anticipation God to accept this « Chalice of Salvation » because at the Consecration it will be filled with the Blood of Him Who is « propitiation for our sins and for those of the whole world » (I John. 2, 2).

Offerimus tibi... *We offer unto Thee, o Lord, the Chalice of Salvation, entreating Thy mercy, that, in the sight of Thy divine Majesty, it may ascend with sweet fragrance for our salvation, and for that of the whole world. Amen.*

Here again (cf. p. 49) we have thoughts and terms exactly similar to the prayers of offering contained in the Canon. Let us notice the striking parallelism between this *Offerimus tibi*, and the *Supra quæ* and the *Supplices* (p. 87) that follow the Consecration. On both occasions the sacrifices of the Patriarchs are mentioned, and, with an almost identical symbolical language, it is asked that the offering may « ascend to the presence of the Divine Majesty ». Here the allusion is to the sacrifice of Noah *(top picture)* : « and the Lord smelled a sweet savour... *odorem suavitatis* » (Gen. VIII, 21) and in the Canon to the sacrifices of Abel, Abraham and Melchisedech, which also foreshadowed the sacrifice of the Last Supper and of Calvary, now offered on the altar. The words « *cum odore suavitatis* » of the oblation of the chalice are emphasized by a sacramental at High Mass : the incensing of the bread and wine ; and the accompanying words speak of an Angel who sends up to God our prayers and offerings as clouds of sweet savour, whilst graces descend on us like an incense cloud. Also the *Supplices* tells of an Angel fulfilling a similar role.

At both times there is an effort to acquire the same spiritual dispositions as the Patriarchs, and the prayers strike a particularly imploring note. Indeed, though Jesus, the principal offerer, although invisible, is always accepted by his Father *in odorem suavitatis (Eph. 5, 2)* this does not apply in the same way to the faithful, in whose name the Church offers the sacrifice, any more than it does to her ministers who, as secondary priests or the instruments of Christ, cause his priesthood to function at the altar.

But, it may be asked, is it not precisely because we are sinners that the sacrifice of the Mass, which is specifically intercessory, is offered ? Is not God particularly attentive to Calvary placed before him in this way, overflowing with the merits of the Blood of the Man-God ? The dispositions of the celebrant and of all those for whom Mass is celebrated add nothing that is essential to the infinite value of the Redemption which is thus

OFFERIMUS TIBI: *(Top)* Noah after the flood offers a sacrifice of thanks to God his deliverer, Who takes pleasure in its « sweet fragrance ». — *(Altar)* The priest, in the middle, lifts up the chalice *(inset)* saying: *Offerimus tibi calicem* (in the plural, as at High Mass the deacon says it with him) and asks God to accept it in « an odour of sweetness ». In remembrance of the Passion he makes the sign of the Cross on the corporal with the chalice which he then places upon it *(inset)*.

offered. For as the Council of Trent reminds us — alluding to the verse of Genesis: « Melchisedech the king of Salem, bringing forth bread and wine, for he was the priest of the most high God » (Gen. 14, 18) — at the Last Supper, Christ, a priest for ever according to the order of Melchisedech (Ps. 109, 4) offered to his Father under the species of bread and wine his Body and Blood » (Sess. 22) and at Mass he repeats this offering by the agency of those who, by the Sacrament of Order, participate in this same priesthood.

The whole course of tradition supplies the answer : since Jesus entrusted his Eucharistic sacrifice to the Church and it is applied to the members of the Church, God wills that priest and people should, by their generosity, co-operate in this putting into effect of the Redemption of which they are the beneficiaries.

« Surprising as it may seem, » says Pius XII, « Christ desires to be aided by the members of his Mystical Body in the accomplishment of his work of Redemption. Obviously this is not because of anything lacking in him or of his weakness but rather that for the honour of his Bride, the Church, he has so arranged matters. »

17. IN SPIRITU — 18. VENI SANCTIFICATOR.

The Church, after having prepared and placed on the altar the materials for the sacrifice, continues to prepare our souls so that they shall have the same sentiments as Christ when he accomplished the mystery of our Redemption.

Saint Augustine says : « The visible sacrifice is the sacrament or sacred sign of the invisible sacrifice. Therefore the prophet, and the penitent soul which he represents, appealing to God for mercy, say : The true sacrifice is a soul broken by sorrow ; you will not disdain, o Lord, a contrite and humble heart ». (De Civ. Dei, L. 10, 5 and in Ps. 4).

Likewise St Gregory : « It is necessary that, when we accomplish this sacrifice, we immolate ourselves to God by a contrite heart ; because, when we celebrate the mystery of the Passion of the Lord, we must live what we are doing. Jesus only becomes a true Victim for us before the Face of His Father, when we, entering into His dispositions, become victims ourselves » (Dial. L. IV, c. 59).

The two prayers that the priest says at this moment are inspired by similar thoughts.

LAVABO: *(Top)* King David in exile composes the 25th Psalm in which he yearns to return to Jerusalem, to be able to praise God in the Temple. — *(Altar)* The priest goes to the right hand side. The server, who has fetched the water cruet, a dish and the lavabo towel *(altar)*, pours some water on the fingers of the priest *(inset)*, who says the 25th Psalm, beginning from verset 6: *Lavabo inter innocentes*, and wipes his fingers on the towel.

The first is the one the three young Hebrews said when offering themselves up as victims in the furnace :

In spiritu ... *In a humble spirit, and with a contrite heart,
may we be received by Thee, O Lord,*
*and may our sacrifice so be offered up in Thy sight this day,
that it may be pleasing to Thee, O Lord God.*

The second prayer asks God to consecrate our offerings through the Holy Ghost and to sanctify our hearts, so that He will be glorified by the gift which we are offering Him and by the manner in which we offer it.

Veni .. *Veni, Sanctificator* ... *Come, Sanctifier, almighty and eternal God,*
and bless † this sacrifice, prepared for Thy holy name.

19. LAVABO : Prayers and purification.

The priest, out of respect, washes the fingers that are going to touch the holy species *(altar and inset)* and he says a part of the 25th Psalm. This ceremony is a sacramental that purifies our souls in the measure in which we take part in it by those good interior dispositions (contrition, confidence, etc...) which it aims to arouse in us. Let us proclaim with David *(top picture)* our wish to glorify God in His Temple, at His altar and in the holy assemblies. Let us ask to be delivered from those who sin and who offend justice by allowing themselves to be bribed.

Lavabo... *I will wash my hands among the innocents and will compass Thy altar, O Lord.*
That I may hear the voice of Thy praise, and tell of all Thy wondrous works.
O Lord, I have loved the beauty of Thy house, and the place where Thy glory dwelleth.
Destroy not my soul with the wicked, O God, nor my life with men of blood.
In whose hands are iniquities : their right hand is filled with gifts.
But I have walked in mine innocence : redeem me and have mercy on me.
My foot hath stood in the straight way : in the churches I will bless Thee, O Lord.
Glory be to the Father, and to the Son and to the Holy Ghost, as it was in the beginning, is now and ever shall be, world without end. Amen.

SUSCIPE SANCTA TRINITAS: *(Top)* The Holy Trinity, Our Lady, St John the Baptist, St Peter, St Paul and all the heavenly host who are spoken of in this prayer. — *(Altar)* The celebrant in the middle, bows and rests his joined hands on the edge of the altar, saying the Suscipe (inset). The word *istorum* (these, see page 61) refers to the relics of the Saints enclosed in the altar, to show their participation, as members of Christ, in the oblation of their Head.

20. SUSCIPE SANCTA TRINITAS : Honour to God and to His Saints.

Suscipe ... *Receive, O Holy Trinity, this offering, which we make to Thee, in remembrance of the Passion, Resurrection and Ascension of our Lord Jesus Christ and in honour of Blessed Mary ever Virgin, of Blessed John the Baptist, of the holy Apostles Peter and Paul, of these (whose relics are enclosed in the altar) and of all the Saints : that it may avail to their honour and our salvation : and may they vouchsafe to intercede for us in Heaven, whose memory we celebrate on earth. Through the same Christ our Lord. Amen.*

The virtue of religion, and the sacrifice which is its principal act, have God as final end. And as God is one Nature and three Persons, it is to the Holy Trinity that the Church makes the Eucharistic oblation. The *Suscipe Sancte Pater* (p. 49) was addressed to the Father, as the Begetter of the Son, and as having given to the Son power in His turn to be, with Him, co-principle of the Holy Ghost. The *Suscipe Sancta Trinitas (altar and inset)* is addressed to the three Persons who possess, under different titles (the Father, *a se* ; the Son, *a Patre* ; the Holy Ghost, *ab utroque)* the same and indivisible Divine Nature.

The Holy Trinity is particularly honoured at the altar because the Mass is a reminder of, and puts into effect, the mystery of Redemption in which the three Divine Persons cooperate. For, after winning for the God-Man, Head of the new humanity, His complete victory over the devil on Good Friday, over death on Easter day and over the world on the Ascension, They work unceasingly and especially through the Holy Sacrifice, to make all men of good will participate in this same victory and attain to this same triumph, first in their souls and then in their bodies.

St Paul says : « But God who is rich in mercy for his exceeding charity wherewith He loved us even when we were dead in sins, hath quickened us together in Christ (by Whose grace you are saved), and hath raised us up together and made us sit in the heavenly places, through Jesus Christ, that He might show in the ages to come the abundant riches of His grace in His bounty towards us in Christ Jesus... for by Him we have access both in one Spirit to the Father ». (Eph. II, 4-7, 18).

The Mass reminds us of the Passion or immolation of Jesus Christ by the sacramental renewal of it, and it recalls the memory of His Resurrection and Ascension. We know that it is the risen and glorious Christ Who is indeed present under the holy species.

The mysteries by which Christ brought about and consummated our Redemption, are recalled for the purpose of applying their healing and sanctifying virtue to the members of the Mystical Body. Thus they can take to themselves that which their Head has done for them and then, in their turn, glorify God. We enter by faith and love into union with the Victim, Who is a *living* Victim. In this way do we all the more truly die to ourselves in His death, and rise to a new and heavenly life in His Resurrection and Ascension, for each of these mysteries produces its own effect. (Roman Catechism, Symbol, C. 6 and 7).

The Church then quotes the names of certain saints, the same as those mentioned in the *Confiteor (top picture* p. 20 and p. 21) and in the *Oramus te, Domine* (p. 24) ; that is to say: the Blessed Virgin Mary, St John the Baptist, the Apostles Peter and Paul, the Saints venerated there because their relics are in the altar, and all the Saints.

Jesus intimately joins the Saints, now His glorious members, with these mysteries, and rewards their generosity by letting them take part with Him in applying these mysteries to our souls. We have recourse to their intercession, counting, as they do, on the merits of Christ, *per eumdem Christum*. And the Saints are summoned thus to be honoured, both for the courage with which they witnessed for Jesus while in the world, and for their power now that they are in Heaven, where they work together with their Head for our salvation, by virtue of their past merits and of their present prayers.

21. ORATE FRATRES — 22. SECRET : Conclusion of the Offertory.
See illustration, p. 64.

The priest at the beginning of the Offertory, after the *Dominus vobiscum*, exhorted the faithful to prayer : *Oremus*. He now repeats this invitation with the *Orate Fratres (altar)*. The greeting *(Dominus vobiscum)* and this invitation *(Orate)* are preceded by the kissing of the altar *(inset)* as it is in Christ's name that the celebrant acts.

Orate, fratres ... *Brethren, pray that my sacrifice and yours may be acceptable to God the Father Almighty.*

The priest addresses all, and all should reply, at least with their heart:

Suscipiat ... *May the Lord receive the sacrifice of thy hands to the praise and glory of His name, to our benefit, and to that of all His holy Church.*

The Apostle says : « God, the Father of our Lord Jesus Christ, predestinated us unto the adoption of children through Jesus Christ *unto the praise of the glory of His grace*, for by Him we have access both in one Spirit to the Father. Now therefore you are no more strangers and foreigners : but you are fellow-citizens with the Saints and the domestics of God » *(Eph.* I, 3-6; II, 18-19).

It follows that Christians are all brothers in Jesus Christ *(fratres)* and all, united with Him, turn now to God as towards their Father *(Deum Patrem)*.

It is above all at the Holy Sacrifice that this fraternal union makes itself felt ; as begun on Calvary, nothing fortifies it more than Calvary continued on the altar. Also nothing adds more « unto the praise and the glory » of the goodness of God as a Father, and to the salvation of all His adopted children, than this sacrificial meal. For here the Son of God, Who is their elder brother, sets them free by virtue of his blood, and strengthens the ties of their Christian brotherhood and of their divine sonship. Therefore each member of the Mystical Body of Christ, and thus the entire holy Church of God *(totiusque Ecclesiae suae sanctae)*, scattered all over the world, benefits from each Mass *(top picture)*.

ORATE FRATRES: *(Top)* Map showing the whole world, in which 350.000 Masses are celebrated daily, « to the praise and glory of God's name », and « for the benefit of His holy Church » spread throughout the world. — *(Altar)* After kissing the altar, which represents Jesus Christ *(inset)*, the priest turns round towards the congregation and with arms extended exhorts them to associate themselves with the sacrifice which they have in common.

The **Orate fratres** shows also that the priest at the altar is a mediator, and that the faithful must unite themselves to his sacrifice, which is also theirs *(meum ac vestrum sacrificium)* because they offer it through him *(manibus tuis)* inasmuch as he is a minister of Christ and His Church.

Saint Paul says : « One mediator of God and men, the man Christ Jesus who gave himself a redemption for all » (I Tim. II, 5-6). The Church points out this mediation by putting on the altar, through the medium of the priest, the offerings that represent us. « The altar of the Holy Church », says the Pontifical, « is Jesus Christ himself, according to the testimony of St. John in the Apocalypse, who saw an altar of gold before the throne of God, for in Him and by Him the gifts of the faithful are offered » (Ordination of sub-deacons).

It belongs to the God-Man alone to immolate Himself in sacrifice and offer us with Him. This He did on the Cross when He died for us all, and this He continues to do at Mass, as invisible mediator, through the ministry of the visible Church. So that through the hands of the priest lifting up the paten and offering the sacrifice, we offer up Jesus Christ and ourselves *(see inset p. 50)* ; otherwise it would be an act of private devotion. Jesus, the Priest and Victim of Calvary, actually offers Himself up at the altar through the priests, to enable us to associate ourselves more intimately, by sacrifice ever more generously offered, with His redeeming oblation, which gives so much glory to God and is so beneficial to souls.

The **Secret** is a prayer of oblation and ends the Offertory. By saying *Amen* with all our heart we will make completely ours the whole of the Offertory.

PREFACE: *(Top)* In unity with the God-Man all the choirs of Angels hymn with transports of joy the glory of God in Three Persons, — *(Altar)* The priest invites all present to raise their thoughts to Heaven; and, clasping his hands in a gesture of supplication *(inset)* he calls upon the faithful to give thanks to God. Raising his hands facing one another, he says the Preface, and begs that we too may be allowed to join with the angelic choir in saying the *Sanctus*.

2. CONSUMMATION OF THE SACRIFICE :
From the Preface to the Lord's Prayer

23. PREFACE — 24. SANCTUS : Prelude to the Eucharistic Prayer.

At the *Preface* the Church, in imitation of Jesus at the Last Supper, says a prayer of thanksgiving, followed by petition (see p. 73). Then she renews, by the consecration of the bread and wine, what Bossuet describes as « the action in which Christ, separating His Body and His Blood by the power of His word, shows Himself before the eyes of Almighty God under a symbol of death and burial ; honouring Him thus as Lord of Life and death, and acknowledging in a supreme manner His sovereign Majesty in presenting before the Divine Eyes that most perfect obedience which extended even to the death of the cross » (Explanation of the Mass).

This Eucharistic oblation has for its end the uniting of all the members of Christ on earth with that Offering which He, their Head, made of Himself at the Last Supper and on Calvary, and which He consummates gloriously in Heaven with the Elect ; as it is written : « I will not drink from henceforth of this fruit of the vine until that day when I shall drink it with you new in the Kingdom of my Father ». (Matt. XXVI, 29).

Thus the Church raises our souls to the heavenly regions :

V/ **Dominus vobiscum** : *The Lord be with you.* — R/ *And with thy spirit.*

V/ **Sursum corda** : *Lift up your hearts.* — R. / *We lift them up unto the Lord.*

V/ **Gratias agamus** : *Let us give thanks unto the Lord.* — R/ *It is right and just so to do* (see inset).

And she concludes the Preface by showing us that all the Angels form part of the Mystical Body of Christ and praise God in union with their Leader :

« **Per quem laudant Angeli** ... *Through Whom the Angels praise Thy majesty, the Dominions worship it, and the Powers are in awe. The heavens and the heavenly host, and the blessed Seraphim join together in celebrating their joy* » (top picture).

Then the liturgy recalls the vision in which Isaias heard the chanting of the Seraphim.

SANCTUS — BENEDICTUS: *(Top)* Isaias sees and hears the Seraphim round the throne of God *(see also top of p. 66)*; they cry one to the other « *Sanctus* ». — The Thrice Holy God sent upon earth the God-Man, Who was acclaimed by the Hebrew children on His entry into Jerusalem. — *(Altar)* The priest, bowing low, says the SANCTUS. He raises himself, and says the BENEDICTUS, signing himself with sign of the Cross *(inset)*, because it is by the Cross that Jesus has saved us.

« **Sanctus** ... *Holy, Holy, Holy is the Lord, the God of hosts (or, of the Heavenly armies). The earth is filled with His glory* » (Is. VI, 3). The words « Heaven, and » have been added to « earth », because the great High Priest of the glory of God is there also and reigns over the angelic choirs. And the Church implores God to allow us to join our voices to theirs, that He may be glorified here below as He is in Heaven.

The Canon of the Mass begins after the « *Benedictus* » by those intercessory prayers which are continued after the Consecration *(see table, p. 15, N^{rs} 26 to 30 and 36 & 37)*, and which join together, in the Communion of Saints, all the members of the Church — militant, triumphant and suffering — to that oblation which Jesus makes unceasingly of Himself in Heaven, and upon the altars of the Church, where nearly 350.000 Masses are celebrated day by day.

The prayers of the Canon are concluded by a solemn doxology, at which point the Church, taking into her hands the Body and Blood of Jesus Christ, shows Them, saying : « By Him and with Him and in Him, is all honour and glory to Thee, God the Father almighty, in the unity of the Holy Ghost, for ever and ever. Amen ».

The whole of this thanksgiving, particularly the *Preface*, which is its prelude, and the final hymn of praise, which completes and resumes the Preface, reproduces those ideas of St. Paul : « Blessed be the God and Father of our Lord J. C., who hath blessed us with spiritual blessings in Christ .. Who hath predestinated us unto the adoption of children through Jesus Christ... » (Eph. I, 3-5.) « In Whom we have redemption through His Blood, the remission of sins, according to the riches of His grace... That He might make known unto us the mystery of His will, according to His good pleasure, which (is)... to re-establish all things in Christ, that are in Heaven (the Angels), and on earth (mankind), in Him... that we may be unto the praise of His glory » (Eph. I, 7-12). « His power which He wrought in Christ, raising Him up from the dead and setting Him on His right hand in the heavenly places, above all principality and power, and virtue and dominion... » (Eph. I, 19-21). « For by Him we have access both in one Spirit to the Father... » (Eph. II, 18). « To Him (the Father) be glory in the Church and in Christ Jesus, unto all generations, world without end... » (Eph. III, 21).

Such is the general outline of the fifteen different Prefaces contained in the Missal.

The origin of the Preface goes back to that Paschal feast which the Jews made each year to celebrate the anniversary of their deliverance from the Egyptian captivity. While eating the symbolic Lamb, the head of each household praised the power, wisdom and kindness of God, which showed itself in His goodness towards His people. He thanked God for the Creation of the world, the safety granted to Noah, the call of Abraham, the passage through the Red Sea, the revelation given on Sinaï, and the conquest of Canaan.

These glorious episodes of the Old Law symbolized the great mysteries of Redemption, of which Christ was the hero. Thus, after having eaten the Paschal Lamb with His Apostles in the Upper Room, Jesus inaugurated the New Law, by immolating and eating the true Lamb of God with a new hymn of thanksgiving: « *Accepto pane gratias egit* » (Luke, XXII, 19) ; « *accipiens calicem, gratias egit* » (Matt. XXVI, 27).

This new Eucharistic prayer took the place of the former thanksgivings. « The priest », says St. Justin, « glorifies the Father of the universe through the name of the Son and of the Holy Spirit ; then he makes a long thanksgiving (eucharistic prayer) for all the benefits we have received through Him. And all sing : *Amen* » (II. century).

In the Preface of Sunday the Church gives glory to God Himself : one in Nature and three in Persons — that is, the mystery of that Triune Life which has been revealed to us by Christ, particularly at the Last Supper. The Preface of the Blessed Trinity approaches most closely to the primitive Eucharistic prayer entirely trinitarian, and preceded in date by a long time the actual Feast of the Blessed Trinity, being already included in the Gelasian Sacramentary.

The Church hymns in the other Prefaces the Blessed Trinity also, but in these cases in Their works : God the Father, almighty, Who has created us and redeemed us through His Son, and Who sanctifies us by making us take a share, through the Holy Spirit, in the Divine Sonship of Jesus Christ.

Vere dignum.. *It is truly meet and just, ... that we should always and in all places give thanks to Thee, holy Lord, Father almighty, everlasting God*, because :

(Christmas) in the Incarnation, we recognize God under a visible form.

(Epiphany) Thine only-begotten Son hath restored our nature by His immortality.

(Lent) Thou dost give us a reward for our bodily fasting, through Christ.

(Passion) Thou hast willed to save the human race through the Tree of the Cross.

(Easter) Christ, by His rising again, hath restored life to us.

(Ascension) Christ hath ascended into Heaven to make us partakers of His divinity.

(Pentecost) seated at Thy right hand, Jesus has sent the Holy Ghost to the children of adoption.

In the same strain the Church gives glory to God because Jesus Christ is present in the Blessed Sacrament (at *Corpus Christi*); because His Love is unchangeable *(Feast of the Sacred Heart)*; because He is Priest and King *(Feast of Christ the King)*; because the Mother of God *(Feasts of the Blessed Virgin)*, the chaste spouse of Mary *(Feasts of St. Joseph)*, the heads of the Church *(Feasts of the Apostles)*, all have a share in the work of Redemption: and finally, because our own death will be followed by resurrection and immortality *(Preface for Masses for the Dead)*.

25. BENEDICTUS.

Thence we sing, with the Angels, who are beholding these wonders, the thrice-holy God *(Sanctus, p. 69)*; following which we praise Jesus-Christ, through Whom God bestows all these blessings on us:

Benedictus ... *Blessed is He Who cometh in the name of the Lord! Hosanna in the highest!* (inset).

This is the cry of praise which Jesus heard on His triumphant entry into Jerusalem, as He was about to conquer the devil through His own death on the Cross. It leads us on to that moment when the self-same Christ will come upon the Altar, and let us take a share in His death and His victory *(top picture)*.

TE IGITUR — MEMENTO — COMMUNICANTES: *(Top)* Heaven, where Mary, the Apostles (12 are mentioned), the Martyrs (12 of these mentioned also) and all the other Saints are praying to God for us. — *(Altar)* After reciting the *Te igitur*, kissing the altar (when he has pronounced the name Jesus) and making three signs of the Cross over the bread and wine to be consecrated, the priest says the *Memento of the Living* with hands joined *(inset)*, and the *Communicantes*.

26. TE IGITUR — 27. 1st MEMENTO — 28. COMMUNICANTES :
Prayers for the Church.

The whole work of the Redemption is centred in the sacrifice which Jesus offered in a sacramental manner in the midst of the Apostles at the Last Supper, which He performed in a bloody manner before Mary His mother and St John on Calvary, which He renews in a Eucharistic manner through the successors of the Apostles and the priests, with whom the faithful unite themselves, and which He consummates in glory with the Angels and Saints in Heaven, displaying to the Father his glorious wounds.

All these offerings, of which Jesus is the High Priest and the Victim, have one end, which our Saviour explained at the Last Supper when He said « I sanctify myself (i.e. I offer Myself)... that they all may be one » (St. John. XVII, 19, 21).

This Unity is that of the Mystical Body, a living organism of which the Head is the Son of God and the members are all mankind on earth, in Heaven or in purgatory, who, like children of adoption, can, through Jesus, with Jesus and in Jesus, approach God as a Father.

The fruit of the Sacrifice of the Cross, this union of Christ and His Church, is realized then in a special way at the altar, where Jesus perpetuates for this end the sacrifice of Calvary through the priests of His Church. The Roman Canon therefore has framed the sacrificial Eucharistic act or Consecration with five prayers (3 before and 2 after), which make special mention of the communion which exists between the Church militant in general (*Te igitur* below) or in particular (*1st Memento* below), the Church triumphant (*Communicantes*, below — *Nobis quoque* p. 93) and the Church suffering (*2nd Memento* p. 89).

It is through Jesus, as the Preface says, that the angels, with whom our voices are joined, praise God. So the Canon (or the Rule to be followed in celebrating) begins with that prayer.

Te igitur ... *We therefore humbly pray and beseech Thee, most merciful Father, through Jesus Christ Thy Son and our Lord, that Thou wouldst accept and bless these † gifts and † offerings, this holy and unblemished † sacrifice, which we offer to Thee in the first place for Thy holy Catholic Church : may it please*

HANC IGITUR — QUAM OBLATIONEM : *(Top)* A priest of the Old Law stretches his hands over a victim to show that in the name of the people, whom it is thus representing, he offers it to God, in Whose honour he is going to sacrifice it. — *(Altar)* The priest stretches his hands over the bread and wine to show that they represent us. In order that this offering of ourselves may be acceptable, he prays God to change the bread into the Body and the wine into the Blood of Jesus *(inset)*.

Thee to grant her peace, to protect and unify her and govern her throughout the world.

It is in communion with the Pope, the pontiff of the universal Church, and with the Bishop, the pontiff of the diocesan Church, that priests celebrate. And the celebrant continues : *We offer this sacrifice in communion with thy servant N... our Pope, with N... our bishop and all the (venerable bishops,* adds the Liturgy of St James) *true believers and all who profess the Catholic and apostolic faith.* Then the priest recommends to God those who are going to celebrate Mass or who are present at it.

Memento ... *Be mindful, Lord, of Thy servants and handmaids N..., N... and of all here present whose faith and devotion (virtue of religion) are known to Thee, for whom we offer or who offer to Thee this Sacrifice of praise (Ps. XLIX, 23), for themselves and for their neighbours, for the redemption of their souls, for the hope of their salvation and safety ; who now render homage to Thee, everlasting God, living and true* (inset).

May God accept our sacrifice in virtue of the merits of the Saints for they, mystical members of Christ, unite their sufferings and their merits to those of their Head.

Communicantes ... *Sharing in the same communion and keeping the memory first of glorious Mary ever a Virgin, Mother of our God and Lord Jesus Christ and of the blessed Apostles and Martyrs, Peter and Paul, Andrew, James, John, Thomas, James, Philip, Bartholomew, Matthew, Simon and Thaddeus,* — *Linus, Cletus, Clement, Sixtus, Cornelius* (5 Popes, martyrs), *Cyprian* (Bishop martyr), *Laurence* (deacon martyr), *Chrysogonus, John and Paul, Cosmas and Damian* (5 lay martyrs) *and of all Thy Saints, grant us always, through their merits and prayers, the help of Thy protection, through the same Jesus Christ our Lord. Amen.* (Top picture).

29. HANC IGITUR — 30. QUAM OBLATIONEM : May God accomplish the Transubstantiation.

The Thanksgiving which has ceased after the *Benedictus* is going to be continued in the consecration of the Eucharist, one of the ends of which is thanksgiving. The Church prepares for this Consecration by two prayers of offering : *Hanc Igitur* and *Quam oblationem*. The prayer of petition *(Te igitur, 1" Memento, Communicantes,* p. 73-75) will be continued *(2nd Memento* p. 89, *Nobis quoque* p. 93) after the offering of the Victim to God.

Hanc igitur ... *We beseech Thee, O Lord, to receive favourably this offering of Thy servants* (the priests in the plural, alluding to concelebration) *and of Thy whole family* (the faithful) : *ut placatus accipias* (inset).

Towards 600 A.D. St Gregory added : *Order our days in Thy peace, deliver us from eternal damnation, and receive us into the number of Thine elect. Through Christ Our Lord. Amen.*

While saying *Hanc igitur* the priest stretches both his hands over the bread and wine *(inset)*.

In the Old Testament when Victims were offered for sacrifice hands were always laid upon them : Aaron and his sons placed their hands on the head of the ram *(top picture)*; it was killed and Moses poured out the blood and burned the body on the altar. « It was a holocaust of most sweet odour to the Lord. » (See *Leviticus* VIII, 14, 21).

The oldest account of the Mass in any detail, the *Tradition* of the Apostles, describes the holy mysteries celebrated by a bishop : he lays his hands on the oblation. This is a prayer for divine grace to come down upon the Eucharistic offerings.

This rite of the imposition of hands disappeared from the Mass for many centuries. It was restored by Pius V in the sixteenth century to assert the sacrificial nature of the Consecration which was then denied by heretics. While saying the *Quam oblationem* the priest makes three signs of the Cross over the offerings (once they covered the whole altar), then one over the bread when saying *corpus*, and one over the wine when saying *sanguis* to signify that they are to be changed into the *Body* and *Blood* of Christ respectively.

The addition made by St. Gregory comprises the blessings that we hope for from the sacrifice, and which the Church emphasizes in the prayer of intercession : *Te igitur* (peace), *1er Memento* (the Redemption of our souls), *Nobis quoque* (the society of the elect). Peace among men is one of the conditions of the perfect growth of the Church in the world. As for the avoiding of Hell and the gaining of Heaven, that is the essential reason of the sacrifice of Calvary and its renewal on the altar. Thus the Council of Trent says : « After celebrating the ancient Pasch that the multitude of the children of Israel sacrificed in memory of the deliverance from Egypt (type of the salvation of our souls), Jesus constituted Himself the new Pasch that the Church would sacrifice in memory of His passage from this world to His Father, while by the shedding of His blood He redeemed us from the power of darkness and transported us into the Kingdom of light » (SS. XXII).

Quam oblationem ... *This offering, do Thou, O God, vouchsafe in all things to † bless, † consecrate, † approve, make reasonable (rationabilem) and acceptable that it may become for us the † Body and † Blood of Thy most beloved Son our Lord Jesus Christ.*

The Church in this prayer states its express wish to change the *bread* into the *Body* of Christ and the *wine* into His *Blood*; so that the account of the Last Supper which follows is not merely an historical recital as are the Gospels of the Passion in Holy Week.

This offering which represents us, on becoming Jesus Himself, will be truly blessed *(benedictam)* and irrevocably *(ratam)* accepted *(adscriptam, acceptabilem)*. Thus united to Christ Who is going to give Himself to us *(fiat nobis)* we shall be able to « present our bodies a living sacrifice, holy, pleasing to God, our reasonable (spiritual) service » (Rom. XII, 1).

31. QUI PRIDIE : Transubstantiation of the bread into the Body of Jesus.

On coming into the world (Hebr. X, 5) and throughout his life Jesus offered Himself to His Father ; but this offering only became a true sacrifice when expressed by an exterior sacrificial act. This sacrificial action, sublime above all others, was twice performed by Jesus in the course of His life on earth : at the Last Supper and on Calvary.

At the Last Supper, supreme High Priest according to the order of Melchisedech, He took bread *(top picture)*, and changed its substance into the substance of *His Body*. Then, at the end of the repast, He took wine, and transubstantiated it also, but this time into *His Blood* to signify by this sacrificial rite, which foreshadowed His death on the Cross, that He was offering His life « *in remissionem peccatorum* ».

On Calvary, a few hours afterwards, High Priest whose sacrifice was prefigured by the bloody sacrifices of Aaron's priesthood, He actually shed, drop by drop, all His blood. And this

QUI PRIDIE: *(Top)* Jesus at the last supper, takes the bread, and after raising His eyes to heaven, He blesses and consecrates it. — *(Altar)* The priest wipes the thumb and first-finger of each hand, takes the host, and after raising his eyes to heaven makes over it the sign of the Cross and pronounces the words of the first consecration *(inset)*. — Then he genuflects, and lifts the consecrated Host for the faithful to adore It. The server lifts the chasuble and rings the bell.

sacrifice was voluntary, because the Son of God, Who could have prevented the tormentors and death from striking Him, freely accepted the death on the Cross. « Christ, says St. Thomas, presented Himself willingly to the Passion, and because of this He is a real Victim ». (III, Qu. 22, art. 2).

The Sacrifice of the Last Supper, of its very essence, refers to the sacrifice of Golgotha, since in the presence of His Apostles, Christ offered in anticipation to His Father, in a eucharistic manner, the offering of Himself which He was going to make on the Cross. The Eucharist, indeed, is above all a *sacrifice offered to God*, and as such is the sacrament or the symbol of the Passion. For in performing two consecutive consecrations, the direct effects of which are different, our divine Saviour carried out eucharistically or representatively (since a sacrament is an outward sign) the separation of His *Blood* from His *Body* that was to take place the next day.

The Last Supper was therefore a true sacrifice where Christ actually made a complete offering of Himself by the rite of the *double* eucharistic consecration, a rite which consisted in offering in anticipation the bloody sacrifice of Calvary, in performing it in a sacramental or unbloody manner. Holy Mass, renewal of the Last Supper, only differs from it in that Jesus performs this *double* transubstantiation through the ministry of His Church and that His priests, who act as instruments of the High Priest, offer sacramentally to God, no longer a Victim who is going to mount His Cross, but the Victim Who has already been offered there. At the altar, says St Paul, « you show the death of the Lord » (I, Cor. XI, 26); for Holy Mass, renewal of the Last Supper, is connected essentially, as was the Last Supper, with the Passion of the Saviour.

Thus, in instituting the Eucharist, Christ left to His Church a visible sacrifice through which, as the instrument of the High Priest of the New Law and at His command she offers with a reality ever new, one and the same sacrifice of redemption. At the Last Supper, on Calvary and in our Churches, it is the same Priest who offers the same Victim by the separation whether physical (Calvary) or sacramental (Last Supper and Mass) of the same Body and the same Blood. Therefore, on the altar, at the moment of the consecration Jesus performs essentially the same priestly and sacrificial action as at the Last Supper and on Golgotha. He continues the same offering of Himself, « the man-

SIMILI MODO: *(Top)* Jesus at the Cenacle takes the chalice, blesses it, and consecrates it. — *(Inset)* The priest makes a sign of the Cross over the wine and pronounces the words of the second consecration. — *(Altar)* He then genuflects and elevates the precious Blood for the adoration of the faithful, while the server lifts the chasuble, and rings the bell. This double elevation recalls to us the separation of the Body and Blood which took place on Calvary.

ner of offering alone is different ». (Conc. Trent. *Sess. XXII*, c. II). Therefore also, the Church at the moment of Consecration reproduces the same gestures and words of Jesus when He consecrated the bread and wine at the Last Supper.

The two forms of Consecration of the Roman Missal are composed of phrases given principally by St. Paul (I Cor. XI), and also by the Evangelists and Tradition :

Qui Pridie ... *Who, the day before He suffered* (the priest purifies his fingers on the corporal) *took bread in His holy and venerable hands* (he takes the host) *and lifting his eyes to Heaven, towards Thee, O God, His all-powerful Father,* (he raises his eyes) *giving thanks to Thee, blessed* (he blesses the host) *broke and gave it to His disciples saying* (inset) : *TAKE AND EAT YE ALL OF THIS, FOR THIS IS MY BODY* ».

32. SIMILI MODO : Transubstantiation of the wine into the Blood of Jesus.

Then the priest consecrates the wine *(inset)* because in order to renew what Jesus did at the Last Supper, the Eucharist must at the same time be the sacrament of the Body and of the Blood of Christ. Though Jesus was entirely present under the species of bread after the first consecration, He only said to His Apostles : « *This is My Body* », thus drawing attention only to the changing of the bread into *His Body* or to the transubstantiation which He was just performing : the Host is strictly speaking the sacrament or the sign of the presence *of the Body* of Christ. A second transubstantiation was therefore needed, that of the wine, so that there might also be the sacrament or the sign of the presence *of the Blood* of Christ. And this Jesus did *(top picture).* Owing to these two modalities of one and the same sacrament, which is the Eucharist, the death of the Saviour is most distinctly portrayed and offered at the altar.

« The Blood consecrated separately from the Body, says St. Thomas, represents in a distinct manner the Passion of Christ, because the separation of the Blood from the Body took place at the Passion » (III. Qu. 78, art. 3). We are here at the very centre of the Holy Sacrifice. (See Introduction, p. 5-7).

Jesus redeemed us by shedding His blood ; the sacramental re-presentation of this bloodshed on our altars must therefore occupy our minds especially during Mass. The second form, more detailed than the first one, emphasizes this :

Simili modo ... *In like manner, after He had supped* (the priest takes the chalice in his hands), *taking also this excellent Chalice into His holy and venerable hands, and giving thanks to Thee, He blessed* (sign of the cross on the wine), *and gave it to His disciples, saying:*

TAKE AND DRINK YE ALL OF THIS, FOR THIS IS THE CHALICE OF MY BLOOD, OF THE NEW AND ETERNAL TESTAMENT : THE MYSTERY OF FAITH : WHICH SHALL BE SHED FOR YOU, AND FOR MANY TO THE REMISSION OF SINS. AS OFTEN AS YE DO THESE THINGS, YE SHALL DO THEM IN REMEMBRANCE OF ME.

As mediator of the Pact which God made with the Israelites on Mount Sinaï, Moses took a cup filled with the blood of victims and sprinkled the people saying : « This is the blood of the Covenant which the Lord hath made with you » (Exodus XXIV, 8).

As mediator of the new and eternal Pact of God with the Christians, Jesus takes in His hands the chalice containing His own Blood *(top picture)*, that Blood which He will shed on Calvary, that which will in future be in all chalices. And He gives this Blood to drink to His Apostles, and through them and their successors to all the faithful, as a witness to their right to the heavenly heritage, and to prepare them for it by purifying them spiritually.

The Last Supper, the Cross, the Mass reveal in a very special way the *Mystery of faith* and of love hidden since all eternity in the bosom of God. This mystery consists in the great mercy of the Father who adopts as His children all those who, in union with His only Son and by virtue of His Blood, die to sin and live again as sons of God.

At the very moment when the Church, by the divine Master's order, offers under the visible signs of bread and wine the *Body* and *Blood* of Jesus, it is essential that we should place all our faith and hope in the sacrifice of Calvary of which the offering, thus renewed, appeases God and causes us ever increasingly to benefit from the resources of the new covenant which the death of our Saviour has made effective (*Hebr.* IX, 17).

« Jesus was himself the new Pasch, » says the Council of Trent, « that the Church was to offer by the ministry of his priests in a sacrificial rite under visible signs in memory of his passage through this world to his Father on the day when, by the outpouring of his Blood he redeemed us, snatched us from the powers of darkness and transferred us to his kingdom ».

33. UNDE ET MEMORES : Oblation of the Victim sacramentally immolated.
See illustration, p. 84.

St Paul says that after each of these two consecrations, Jesus declared : « Do this for a commemoration of me » (1 Cor. XI, 24-5). The Church recalls this repeated command by saying after the second consecration « As often as ye shall do these things, ye shall do them in memory of me ».

It is by order of Jesus that the Church renews the sacrifice of the Last Supper, and that she evokes, in so doing, the mysteries by which the Saviour brought about and consummated the Redemption. The priest continues : Wherefore, O Lord, *calling to mind (top picture), we offer (inset)*. These are the two actions of the Church at this moment.

Unde et memores ... *Wherefore, O Lord, we Thy servants, as also Thy holy people, calling to mind the blessed Passion of the same Christ Thy Son our Lord, His Resurrection from the dead, and His glorious Ascension into Heaven, offer unto Thy most excellent Majesty, of Thy gifts and presents, a pure † Host, a holy † Host, a spotless † Host, the holy † Bread of eternal life, and the Chalice † of everlasting salvation.*

After having immolated sacramentally the Victim on the altar, the Church offers It to God. This is the essential aim of this prayer *(Unde et memores)* and the two following ones *(Supra quae, Supplices)* which constitute a whole, as pointed out in old liturgies and demonstrated by the one ending : *Through the same Christ our Lord. Amen* (bottom of page 89).

The *Unde et memores* is also a commentary and a putting into practice of our Lord's instructions to His Apostles : « *As often as ye do these things, ye shall do them in remembrance of Me* ». These instructions given by Jesus when he was about to die and return to His Father, and which the Church repeats after the second form of the Consecration (p. 82) may be interpreted as follows :

I am instituting this Eucharistic rite, and I make you its minis-

UNDE ET MEMORES: *(Top)* Death, Resurrection, Ascension of Jesus. — *(Altar)* The priest, arms extended. *(Inset)* After having said: *Offerimus* (we offer Thee), he makes three signs of the Cross on the Bread and the Wine which he terms a pure Host, a spotless Host, because Christ Who died, rose again, and is in Heaven, is in the Host. Then he makes a sign of the Cross separately on the Host called Holy Bread of eternal life, and on the Chalice, called Chalice of Salvation; this in order to draw attention to the two transubstantiations.

ters so that I may continue through you, who are vowed to My service as priests *(nos servi tui)*, the work of the redemption of the human race ; because the Father sent Me so that I might bring back to Him all His prodigal children by making them members of My Mystical Body *(sed et plebs tua sancta)*.

This work of salvation and sanctification I shall accomplish as Leader of the whole of humanity, because by My death on the Cross I shall expiate the sins of all men, and by My Resurrection and Ascension I shall lead them by right into the kingdom of My Father *(see top picture which shows these three steps)*.

However, all souls who have begun to realize, by becoming My members through Baptism, these mysteries of My Passion, of My Resurrection and My Ascension, must communicate more and more at the celebration of these mysteries by means of the *Eucharistic Sacrifice*. I shall then, I who am the pure Host, the holy Host and the spotless Host, be able more and more to offer them together with Me to the Father as hosts which My Blood purifies, My Resurrection sanctifies and My Ascension brings to heavenly life.

Repeat what I have just done : i. e. offer Me to the Father by consecrating the bread and the wine ; and thereafter make My holy people with this oblation into one Mystical Body, by giving them to eat this holy Bread of eternal life, and making them drink the Chalice of eternal salvation.

Let us add that by thus offering to God His own natural and supernatural gifts : the bread and wine transubstantiated into the Body and Blood of Jesus, the Church pays honour to the Supreme Majesty of Him, Who is at the same time our Creator and Providence in the natural world, as well as our Father and our Benefactor in the supernatural world. And she does it in a manner which infinitely pleases God, because it is the Son of God who thus offers Himself through her. Jesus Christ, says St. Paul, is pre-eminently « a high-priest, holy, innocent, undefiled » (Hebr. VII, 26), and His oblation, adds the Church, is pre-eminently « a pure Host, a holy Host, a spotless Host ». This sacrifice will therefore be pleasing to God.

SUPRA QUÆ: *(Top)* Allegorical figures of Calvary and the Last Supper: Abel offers his best lamb; Abraham, his son Isaac; Melchisedech, bread and wine. — SUPPLICES: *(Top)* The heavenly altar with the Lamb, symbol of Christ in Heaven. — *(Altar)* The priest bowing profoundly. *(Inset)* Hands on the altar. Sign of the Cross on the Bread called *Corpus* and on the Wine called *Sanguis*, to draw attention to the fact that they have been transubstantiated respectively into the *Body* and *Blood* of Jesus.

34. SUPRA QUÆ — 35. SUPPLICES : Acceptance of the Victim by God.

It is not sufficient for the offering of Calvary to be renewed for God to accept it and bestow his favours upon us. In fact He lays down certain conditions, for He desires that men who were saved, without any merit on their part when Jesus redeemed them on the cross, should participate in the sacrifice of their Head when it comes to applying its fruits.

One of the ends of sacrifice is to make satisfaction for sins which have been committed, to liquidate the debt owing to divine Justice. « In making satisfaction », says St Thomas, « it is the loving intention of the offerer that is considered, rather than the size of the offering. Consequently, although this offering (of the Eucharistic sacrifice) of its own value is sufficient to make satisfaction for all punishment (due to sin), yet it is made to satisfy on behalf of those for whom it is offered, and also of those who offer it, according to the extent of their devotion ». (III, q. 79, a. 5) And he adds : « This sacrifice is to be preferred to all the sacrifices of old ; and yet the sacrifices of the Old Testament fathers were very acceptable to God on account of their devotion. The priest asks therefore that this sacrifice be accepted by God on account of the devotion of those who offer it, even as the sacrifices of old were accepted by God ». (III, q. 79, a. 4, ad 8)

Generally speaking it can be said that the Mass produces its saving effects in favour of man to the same degree that his interior dispositions resemble those of the divine Victim when he died for us upon the cross.

And the Church shows her ardent desire to have this disposition by naming the three great sacrificers who were, in the highest degree, by their person, by their gifts, and by their generous devotion, the prototypes of Christ Sacrificer and Host *(top)*.

Supra quae ... *Upon which vouchsafe to look with a propitious and serene countenance, and to accept them, as Thou wast graciously pleased to accept the gifts of Thy just servant Abel, and the sacrifice of our patriarch Abraham, and that which Thy high priest, Melchisedech, offered to Thee, a holy sacrifice (bread) and spotless victim (wine).*

MEMENTO OF THE DEAD: *(Top)* The liturgy of the dead sings: « May the Angels lead thee into Paradise ». The Angels fill this role very specially during the Holy Sacrifice which brings such comfort and deliverance to the dead. — *(Altar)* As for the Memento of the Living the priest joins his hands, and names those whom he recommends to God, but in this case the fingers (thumb and forefinger) which have touched the consecrated Host remain joined *(compare inset page 72).*

The offering which Christ makes of Himself through His priests at the altar is identical with that which the same Lamb « as it were slain » (Apoc. V, 6) makes, in union with all the Saints, on the heavenly altar before the throne of the Divine Majesty *(top)*.

Here again, God can only find this sacrifice pleasing in so far as we offer ourselves really with Christ, as do all the members of His Mystical Body, the Angels and Saints in the heavenly Jerusalem.

Further, recalling the vision of the Angel, on the right hand of the golden altar who offers to God like fragrant incense the prayers of the Saints (Apocalypse VIII, 3-4), the priest, bowing profoundly *(inset)* asks in symbolical language, similar to that used at the offering of the chalice (see p. 54) and the incensing of the offerings at the offertory (ibid.), that through the ministry of the Angel watching over the Holy Sacrifice this oblation may be united to that being made in Heaven. Like unto a new Ascension of Christ, this oblation obtains for us the gifts of the Holy Ghost through an inward Pentecost.

This petition, therefore, strengthened by the merits of Christ, *per eundem Christum Dominum nostrum*, present on the two altars simultaneously assures abundant grace to those who will participate through Communion (the priest kisses the earthly altar, symbol of the heavenly altar) at the sacrifice thus made pleasing to God in Heaven.

Supplices ... *We most humbly beseech Thee, almighty God, to command these things to be carried (haec perferri) by the hands of Thy holy Angel to Thine altar on high, in the sight of Thy divine Majesty, that as many as shall partake of the most sacred Body † and Blood † of Thy Son at this altar (he kisses it), may be filled with every heavenly grace and blessing. Through the same Christ our Lord. Amen.*

36. MEMENTO OF THE DEAD : Application of the sacrifice to the Church suffering.

Before the Consecration, the Church had interrupted the prayer of thanksgiving *(Preface, Sanctus,* p. 67, *Benedictus,* p. 71) by a prayer of intercession *(Te igitur, First Memento, Communicantes,* p. 73) which is another way of proclaiming the benefits of the Redemption. After the Consecration, the Eucharistic Action *(Qui pridie, Simili modo, Unde et memores, Supra quae, Supplices,*

p. 81 to p. 89) is again interrupted by two intercessions *(Second Memento*, p. 89, *Nobis quoque peccatoribus*, p. 93) which also praise the goodness of Him Who calls us to eternal happiness.

The Church militant, suffering and triumphant, being the Bride or the Mystical Body of Christ, all His members, vitally united to their Head, may benefit by the Sacrifice which Jesus unceasingly offers through the ministry of His priests at the altar.

From the earliest times, all the liturgies have mentioned at Mass, not only the living and the Saints, but also the dead. The reason given for this by St. Augustine (end of the fourth century) is precisely that « the souls of the faithful departed are not separated from the Church and are members of Christ » *(De Civ. Dei 1, X c. 9).*

Memento etiam ... *Be mindful, O Lord, also* (for this *Memento of the Dead* is linked with that of the living p. 73) *of Thy servants, N. and N., who are gone before us with the sign of faith, and rest in the sleep of peace.*

To these, O Lord, and to all that sleep in Christ, grant, we beseech Thee, a place of refreshment, light, and peace ; through the same Christ our Lord. Amen.

In order to draw attention to the fact that the *Memento of the Dead* is made in favour of the members of Christ, the oriental liturgies say : « Remember Thou, O Lord, those who have been clad with Thee at baptism, and have received Thee at the altar » (West Syrian Office) ; « those who have received the precious Body and Blood of Thy only-begotten Son and have been baptized by His sign » (Anaphora of St. John).

And the *Second Memento* of the Roman Missal *(altar and inset)* says: « Be mindful, O Lord, of Thy servants who have gone before us *with the sign of faith* », which recalls the *First Memento* : « Be mindful, O Lord, of Thy servants, men and women, *whose faith is known unto Thee* ». And he prays for the souls who « sleep in the sleep of peace » and who « rest in Christ ».

In like manner at the Offertory (p. 49) the Church has offered « this spotless host for all faithful Christians, both living and dead, that it may avail them unto life everlasting ».

Having left this world without having made full satisfaction by temporal punishment due for their sins, these souls must purify themselves by expiation until divine justice is fully satisfied, since nothing defiled may enter Heaven. And the sufferings which their sensitive soul, their intelligence and their will endure are referred to when we beg for them « refreshment, light, and peace ».

The Church may shorten the time of their purification. She may do it, says the Council of Trent «especially by the acceptable sacrifice of the altar » *(Sess. XXV)*. As a matter of fact, there is nothing more efficacious for making God propitious to them in regard to the satisfaction of His justice, and for obtaining His mercy *(ut indulgeas deprecamur)* for the remission of their punishment, than to intercede with Him by offering *sacrificially* the blood of Jesus to pay their debts. « The sufferings of the dead for whom Mass is said, or who are specially mentioned by the priest, says St. Gregory, are suspended or lessened during that time » (Dial. VI, 56). How many souls in purgatory are thus comforted or introduced into Heaven by the Angels *(top illustration)* !

The Mass is the best means of bringing to pass for those souls the text of St. Paul : « Christ loved the Church, and delivered Himself up for it : that He might sanctify it, cleansing it by the laver of water in the word of life : that He might present it to Himself, a glorious Church, not having spot or wrinkle or any such thing ; but that it should be holy and without blemish » (Eph. V, 25-27).

NOBIS QUOQUE PECCATORIBUS: *(Top)* The Saints in Heaven (here are mentioned: St. John the Baptist and two series of seven martyrs, men and women). The Precursor is pointing to the Son of God. St. Stephen the deacon in dalmatic is holding his palm. St. Agnes is holding her lamb, St. Cecilia her lyre, St Anastasia her palm. — *(Altar and inset)* The priest strikes his breast and says in a loud voice: *Nobis quoque peccatoribus*, so that all may join him in prayer. He continues with arms extended.

37. NOBIS QUOQUE PECCATORIBUS : Application of the sacrifice to the Church militant.

After having offered the Blood of Christ for the dead, the priest, striking his breast as a sign of contrition *(inset and altar)*, offers it also for us poor sinners. The Church militant and the Church suffering must indeed one day be reunited to the Church triumphant in the Kingdom of Jesus and of His Father.

« Giving thanks », says St. Paul, « to God the Father, Who hath made us worthy to be partakers of *the lot of the saints* in light, Who hath delivered us from the power of darkness, and hath translated us into the kingdom of the Son of His love, in Whom we have redemption *through His blood, the remission of sins* » (Col. I, 12-14).

To ask God, who is infinitely merciful and bountiful *(de multitudine miserationum tuarum ; sed veniae largitor)*, to admit us sinners *(nobis peccatoribus)* who do not deserve it *(non aestimator meriti)* among the elect *(intra quorum consortium)* through the merits of the Blood of Christ *(per Christum Dominum nostrum)*, such is the aim of the *Nobis quoque peccatoribus*, of which the list of Saints continues and completes that given in the *Communicantes* (p. 75).

Nobis quoque peccatoribus ... *Also to us sinners Thy servants, confiding in the multitude of Thy mercies, vouchsafe to grant some part and fellowship with Thy holy Apostles and Martyrs* (top illustration) :

John (the Precursor named first as Our Lady was in the other list p. 75), *Stephen* (deacon), *Matthias* (apostle), *Barnabas* (disciple), *Ignatius* (bishop and martyr), *Alexander* (pope), *Marcellinus* (priest), *Peter* (exorcist), — (i. e. 8 martyrs (men)) — *Felicitas and Perpetua* (Christian mothers), *Agatha* (of Catania), *Lucy* (of Syracuse), *Agnes, Cecilia, Anastasia* (virgins) — (i. e. 7 martyrs (women) *and with all Thy Saints ; into whose company we beseech Thee to admit us, not in consideration of our merit, but of Thine own gratuitous pardon. Through Christ our Lord.*

The Mass being a sacrifice by which Jesus offers anew, without shedding His blood, through the ministry of His priests, the bloody sacrifice consummated on Calvary, this sacramental or Eucharistic oblation has all the propitiatory power of Calvary. Thus the Council of Trent states : « Should anyone say that the sacrifice of the Mass is not a sacrifice of propitiation, let him be anathema ». And the Roman Catechism adds : « The sacrifice of the Mass is a real sacrifice of propitiation which appeases God and renders Him favourable to us. If, therefore, we immolate and offer this most holy Victim with a pure heart, a living faith, and deep sorrow for our sins, we infallibly obtain mercy from the Lord and the help of His grace in all our needs. The fragrancy emanating from this sacrifice is so agreeable to Him that He grants us the gifts of grace and repentance and that He forgives us our sins » (C. 20).

The oblation of the Blood of Christ at the altar is the best means of obtaining *graces of conversion for sinners*, even hardened ones. « Appeased by the offering of this sacrifice », says the Council of Trent, « the Lord grants the grace and gift of penance and forgives crimes and sins, even the greatest » (SS. XXII, c. 2).

Through the Mass we also obtain, if we have contrition, the forgiveness of our *venial sins* : « Jesus Christ at the Last Supper instituted Holy Mass, so that the power of this healing sacrifice may be applied to the forgiveness of our daily faults » (ibid. c. 1).

As to the debt of *punishment due to sin*, this, according to our disposition at that time, is paid to divine justice by this offering of the expiation of Jesus, to which must be added that of the Saints, particularly of those mentioned, and who are thereby glorified because they contribute towards our salvation. « Our Lord Jesus Christ », says the Roman Catechism, « instituted the Eucharist so that the Church should possess a perpetual sacrifice able to *expiate our sins* and through which our Heavenly Father, too often offended in a grievous manner by our iniquity, may change His wrath into mercy and the just severity of His punishment into clemency » (C. 20).

38. PER QUEM — 39. PER IPSUM : Conclusion of the Eucharistic Prayer.

See illustration, p. 96.

The great prayer of thanksgiving, started with the Preface, ends with a formula of glorification, or doxology, similar to those used by St. Paul at the end of his epistles. Speaking of God who calls all men, Jews and Gentiles, to salvation, the Apostle says : « He may have mercy on all, for of him, and by him and in him, are all things : to him be glory for ever, Amen ». (Rom. XI, 32, 36). « Christ Jesus came into this world to save sinners... To the king of ages, immortal, invisible, the only God, be honour and glory for ever and ever. Amen». (I Tim. I, 15, 17). «Grace be to you and peace from God the Father, and from our Lord Jesus Christ, Who gave himself for our sins, that he might deliver us from this present wicked world, according to the will of God and our Father : to whom is glory for ever and ever. Amen ». (Gal. I, 3-5). « To God the only wise », who has revealed to us « the mystery which was kept secret from eternity (of the Redemption), honour and glory through Jesus Christ for ever and ever. Amen » (Rom. XVI, 25, 27).

The Church in her turn, at the altar, after having given thanks to God for the work of Redemption (*Preface* p. 67) and offered Him, through the Eucharistic sacrifice, the same glory which Christ rendered Him at the Last Supper and on Calvary *(Consecration)* and which He continues to give Him in heaven *(Supplices* p. 89), ends the Canon by saying :

Per quem haec omnia ... *Through whom, O Lord, Thou dost always create, sanc†tify, quick † en, bl†ess, and give us all these good things (praestas nobis).*

Per ipsum, et cum ipso, et in ipso ... *Through † Him, and with † Him, and in † Him is to Thee, God the Father almighty, in the unity of the Holy Ghost, all honour and glory. For ever and ever. Amen.*

This doxology is the crowning of the *Action* or of the Eucharistic Mystery, because, as much by its words as by its gestures, it has a bearing on Holy Communion which is the pre-eminent way of participating in the Holy Sacrifice, of receiving abundant

PER QUEM — PER IPSUM : *(Top)* The Holy Trinity. The doxology renders glory to the Father through the Son in the unity of the Holy Ghost. — *(Altar)* The priest ends the Canon with the *Per quem* and the *Per ipsum*. He makes with the Host *(inset)* three signs of the Cross over the chalice, while mentioning three ways of mediation of Jesus (by Him, with Him, through Him) and he names the Father and the Holy Ghost, at the same time making two signs of the Cross away from the chalice, since the Word Incarnate alone has shed His blood. — (The server may ring.)

grace from Jesus, and of glorifying God in an incomparable manner through Jesus.

The *Per quem* is, in fact, the logical conclusion of the *Supplices* (p. 89), wherein the Father was asked to accept our offerings in Heaven *(haec perferri)* and in return to load with His blessings all those who participate at the altar by going to Communion.

The bread and wine *(haec omnia)* were created by God through His Word, and He has in some way re-created them by making them new beings in changing their substance into that of the Body and Blood of the Incarnate Word *(semper bona creas)*. These gifts thus eminently sanctified, quickened, blessed *(sanctificas, vivificas, benedicis)* God has been pleased to accept, since He gives them back to us at Holy Communion *(praestas nobis)*, when they in turn make us into new beings filled with sanctity, life, and blessing.

The *Per ipsum* in its turn was the formula of the fraction, or breaking of the bread, which used to be performed at this moment ; and the gesture of elevation which accompanies this doxology served the purpose of showing simultaneously the Body and Blood of Christ to those who were going to communicate. The priest for this elevation used to touch the rim of the chalice with the consecrated Bread. Hence the three signs of the cross made with the Host over the precious Blood *(inset)*.

The faith and love with which the faithful used to look at this living Host (i. e. the Body and Blood elevated at one and the same time to show that in Christ risen they are not separated) and the Communion, which followed almost immediately, incorporated the members of the Church ever more with their Head. And thus they rendered ever more through Him, with Him and in Him, honour and glory to God the Father in the unity of the Holy Ghost.

Here, as at the end of the Offertory in the case of the oblation, we shall really make our own this sacrifice of glorification by all replying : *Amen.*

PATER NOSTER: *(Top)* Jesus teaches the Our Father to His Apostles. — *(Altar)* The priest lifts his hands and says the Our Father with his eyes on the Host. — *(Inset)* During the *Libera* which develops the seventh request *(see p. 99)*, the priest takes the paten, without separating his thumb from his fore-finger which have both touched the Host, and makes with it a sign of the Cross on himself saying: *da propitius pacem*. Then he kisses this instrument of peace and places the Host upon it, the Host which is « Jesus Who is our peace » (Eph. II, 14).

3. PARTICIPATION IN THE SACRIFICE :
From the Pater noster to the end.

40. THE LORD'S PRAYER : PATER NOSTER.

In all the liturgies of the East and the West, the *Our Father* occurs in the Mass. In Rome it was said after the Breaking of the Host or even after the Communion. S. Gregory considered that it should be, as at the time of the Apostles, brought nearer to the sacrificial act itself *(Ep. XII, 1, 9)* ; for, if the prayer of the Canon composed by the Church is said « over the Body and Blood of the Redeemer », it was fitting that the same should be true of the prayer of which Jesus is the author. Therefore this Pope placed the Lord's Prayer immediately after the Eucharistic prayers, so that it is the first part of the preparation for Communion towards which everything moves from this moment as towards the completion of the sacrifice.

The Lord's Prayer, placed thus between the Consecration and the Communion, plays an important part in the Mass, and shows that we owe our divine sonship to the Blood of Jesus. It is in fact the prayer of all those whom the only Son of God has made members of His Mystical Body — for He has redeemed us, in order « that we might receive the adoption of sons » (Gal. IV, 5) — that is to say, all the baptized have the right and are bound to approach, by Him, with Him and in Him His heavenly Father.

In the Sermon on the Mount *(Matt. VI, 9-13)* and in another instance when one of the disciples asked Jesus : « Lord, teach us to pray » *(Luke XI, 1-4)*, the divine Master replied : « Pray thus ». And he taught them the *Our Father (see top picture)*. Hence the introduction :

Oremus : Praeceptis ... *Let us pray — Instructed by the precepts of salvation, and following the divine institution, we make bold to say.*

In this prayer all the addresses are in the plural and made to God considered as Father :

Pater noster ... *Our Father, who art in Heaven*

1. *Hallowed be Thy name* (on earth as it is in Heaven).

2. *Thy Kingdom come* (on earth as it is in Heaven).

3. *Thy will be done on earth at it is in Heaven.*

4. *Give us this day our daily bread* (for both body and soul).

5. *And forgive us our trespasses as we forgive those who have trespassed against us.*

6. *And lead us not into temptation* (sin).

7. *But deliver us from evil* (the attacks of sin and the Evil one). Amen.

All the assistants take part in this prayer by making this last request, and the priest ends it with the *Amen* of the Gospels *(Mat. VI, 13).*

The *Our Father* is the pre-eminent prayer of the great «household of God» (Ephes II, 19), that is, the prayer that all those whom God has adopted as children in Jesus Christ, make to a common Father for their common interests. These interests concern God first (*Thy* name, *Thy* kingdom, *Thy* will) and afterwards man (give *us*, pardon *us*, lead *us* not, deliver *us*). And these four last requests are connected with the three first, for they indicate the four means (grace and the Eucharist, the forgiveness of sins, the resisting of temptations, the deliverance from penalties due to sin) of doing on earth what the Angels and the Saints do in Heaven ; that is, glorifying or hallowing here on earth the name of God, our Father, by bringing about the universal reign of his Son, by corresponding to the full with the outpourings of the Spirit of Love, and humbly submitting our human wills to the divine will of our heavenly Father.

The whole of the Mass is summed up in the seven points of this prayer, and the Eucharist, as Sacrifice and Sacrament, helps us fully to achieve them. Among other things will be noticed : the similarity of the three first requests with the doxology (p. 63); the object of the fourth request which is especially the Eucharistic bread which the Father gives his children at the Holy Table; the efficacy of the fifth request in obtaining for us the forgiveness of our venial sins, and thus preparing us for Communion.

41. LIBERA NOS — 42. BREAKING OF THE BREAD — 43. PAX DOMINI.

See illustrations, p. 98 and 102.

The priest paraphrases the 7th request. It is the *Libera nos* (see inset p. 98) in which the Saints are invoked (the 4 first of the *Communicantes* p. 75) and in which the hope of peace, placed by St. Gregory in the *Hanc Igitur* (p. 76) is again expressed.

Libera nos ... *Lord, deliver us from all evils past, present and to come, and by the intercession of the blessed and glorious ever Virgin Mother of God,*

of the blessed Apostles Peter and Paul, and of Andrew and of all the Saints,

grant us, in Thy bounty, peace in our days (he signs himself with the paten) *so that, supported by the help of Thy mercy,* (he kisses the paten and places the Host upon it) *we may ever be delivered from sin and freed from all dangers.*

Through the same Jesus Christ, Thy Son, our Lord, who being God liveth and reigneth with Thee in the Unity of the Holy Ghost world without end. Amen.

« The Eucharist is the remedy which frees us from daily faults and preserves us from mortal sin » (Council of Trent. SS. XIII, c. 2). It fortifies us against the evil results of past sin and protects us against the dangers which threaten our future on earth and in eternity. The Saints affirm that, without the Mass, the world could not go on.

In saying the conclusion, the priest *breaks the bread over the chalice (inset).*

This *Breaking of the Bread* is the repetition of what Jesus did at the Last Supper *(see top picture).* « And taking bread into His holy and venerable hands He broke it « *fregit* » (p. 81). This action symbolizes on one hand the sufferings of Christ in His Passion, just as the breaking of unleavened bread at the Pasch expressed the sorrows that the people of God had suffered in Egypt ; and it indicates, on the other hand, that the Christian people must also participate in the sufferings of their Saviour. If Jesus broke the bread, it was, indeed, *to distribute it.* And by

LIBERA — PAX DOMINI — HAEC COMMIXTIO : *(Top)* Jesus breaks bread at the Last Supper. — *(Altar and inset)* In concluding the *Libera*, the priest divides the Host in two over the chalice ; he places on the paten first the right, and then the left half, after breaking off a particle. He makes with this particle three signs of the Cross over the chalice from one edge to the other, saying : *Pax Domini*, and mixes It with the consecrated wine, saying : *Haec commixtio*.

receiving part of this single Host, now broken in pieces, all the Apostles communicated with the Victim who was contained there, and took part in His Passion thus set forth. This conception of Communion as a means of intimately associating all the members with the sacrifice of their Head was that of the early Christians ; thus, the « Acts of the Apostles » say « that they were persevering... in the communication of the breaking of bread and in prayers » (II, 42). « *The bread which we break* says likewise St. Paul, is it not the partaking of the Body of the Lord ? For we, being many, *are one bread, one body*, all that partake *of one bread* » (I Cor. X, 16-17).

The priest makes the sign of the Cross three times with the particle of the Host over the Chalice *(inset)* and says :

V/ **Pax Domini** : *May the peace of the Lord be ever with you.*

R/ *And with thy spirit* (that is, may it enter your soul too).

Formerly, these words preceded the Communion and introduced the *Kiss of Peace* which Christians gave each other in brotherly love at the moment of receiving Jesus and uniting themselves ever more closely to God through Him ; for, says the Apostle, « *God has reconciled us through Christ, making peace through the blood of His Cross* » (Col. I, 20).

The priest then drops the particle of the Host into the precious Blood. Formerly there were two *minglings*. The first was made at this moment with a particle of the Host consecrated at another Mass, as is still done at the Mass of Good Friday. In order to show, indeed, *the unity of the sacrifice* (for all Masses since the Last Supper are a perpetuation of the one unique sacrifice of Calvary), and to assert the *unity of the priesthood* (for all priests celebrate in communion with their Bishop, and all Bishops in communion with the Pope), a part of the Host was reserved, either to be used at the next day's Mass (it was called *Sancta* : sacred things) or to be sent to the Bishop who celebrated in place of the Pope or to the priests who celebrated in the *tituli* or titular churches (then it was called *Fermentum* : leaven of unity and charity). These *Sancta* or *Fermentum*, placed into the chalice at the moment of the *Pax Domini*, were a symbol which expressed the continuity of the sacrifice and the intercommunion of all the priests of Christ.

AGNUS DEI: *(Top)* John the Baptist saw Jesus coming to him and said: « Behold the Lamb of God who taketh away the sins of the world » (John I, 29). John was with two of his disciples and seeing Jesus coming, he said: « Behold the Lamb of God » (John I, 35-36). — *(Altar and inset)* The priest says the *Agnus Dei* and strikes his breast. This is a sign of humility, for Jesus said that the Publican did likewise to humble himself, and that he was justified by his humility.

44. MINGLING — 45. AGNUS DEI — 46. PRAYER BEFORE THE KISS OF PEACE.

The second mingling, made with the Host just consecrated, took place after that of the *Sancta* or the *Fermentum* ; and when the latter usage disappeared, it took its place and kept its symbolical meaning, which was added to its own. Meanwhile, the priest says :

Haec Commixtio ... *May this mingling and consecration of the Body and Blood of our Lord Jesus Christ be to us who receive it an assurance of eternal life. Amen.*

These words proclaim one of the effects which the Eucharist will produce in the soul, for the mingling *(commixtio)* of the consecrated bread and wine *(consecratio)* is an action in preparation for the Communion. Actually, it was sometimes necessary to soak the Hosts in wine in order that they might more easily be absorbed, for they were then coarser than now. Symbolically, this union of the Body and Blood of Christ denotes the mystery of the Resurrection and its life-giving effects « *in vitam aeternam* ». The Resurrection, of which the Mass is a memorial *(Unde et memores* p. 83), is thus symbolized. And indeed, it is the humanity of the risen Jesus which is in the Host, and the same which reigns gloriously in Heaven, and it is a guarantee of ressurrection to those who receive it themselves in Communion.

When the congregation was large, the « Breaking of the Bread », and the « Kiss of peace » occupied a certain time during which the *Agnus Dei* was sung. Hence the triple invocation in which are repeated the words of the Baptist on seeing Jesus *(see top).*

Agnus Dei ... *Lamb of God who takest away the sins of the world, have mercy on us.*

Lamb of God who takest away the sins of the world, have mercy on us. (Cf. p. 104).

Lamb of God, who takest away the sins of the world, grant us peace (see inset).

For the dead : *grant them rest ;* and the third time : *grant them eternal rest.*

This carries us back once again to the Last Supper in which Jesus substituted Himself for the symbolical Lamb. This Lamb was immolated in the Temple and eaten in the houses. After having immolated the true Lamb of God, the Church gives it as a food to souls ; for the altar is, at the same time, the stone of Sacrifice of the New Law, and the table of the true Paschal meal.

As Victim laden with the sins of all men, Jesus has willed to undergo for each of them individually expiatory sufferings which explain the immensity and depth of the pain of his Passion. By his final and heroic victory over the devil, who has lost all his claims on us, Christ has assured the glory of His Father by procuring for men of good will (Cf. Gloria p. 33) peace with themselves (the overcoming of their passions), with their neighbour (union in brotherly love) and with God (reconciliation of the Father with His children). And so, from this moment until the Postcommunion, the Church speaks directly to this divine Saviour and asks Him to give us the peace which He has merited (dona nobis pacem). For the 6th time she expresses this wish.

In an « Oratio ad pacem » such as is found in the Mozarabic liturgy, she recalls again, with the words of Jesus in the Cenacle the peace-giving action of the Eucharist.

Domine Jesu .. *Lord Jesus Christ who hast said to thine Apostles :*

Peace I leave with you, my peace I give unto you (John XIV, 27),

*look not upon my sins but on the faith of Thy Church
and grant her, according to Thy will, peace and unity ;
who livest and reignest God, world without end. Amen.*

At this moment, in solemn Masses, the celebrant kisses the altar close to the Host, and says in the name of Jesus « *Pax tecum* », giving the *kiss of peace* to the deacon, who gives it to the choir, repeating the words « Peace be with you ».

This kiss is the outward sign of divine charity which unites souls, mentioned already in the 5th request of the *Our Father* (see p. 100), and which is at one and the same time the effect of the Eucharist as a Sacrifice and the preparation for the fruitful reception of the Eucharist as a Sacrament : « Go first to be reconciled to thy brother : and then coming thou shalt offer thy gift », the Master has bidden us (Matt. V, 24).

47. PRAYERS BEFORE COMMUNION — 48. DOMINE NON SUM DIGNUS. — 49. COMMUNION.

Before receiving Communion the priest again addresses Christ in two prayers :

The first recalls the words of St. Peter to Jesus : « Thou art the Christ, the Son of the Living God » (Matt. XVI, 16) and the text of St. Paul : « How much more shall the blood of Christ, who by the Holy Ghost offered himself unspotted unto God, cleanse our conscience from dead works (sins), to serve the living God ? » (Hebr. IX, 14).

Domine Jesu Christe ... *Lord Jesus Christ, Son of the Living God, who by the will of the Father and the cooperation of the Holy Ghost*

hast by Thy death given life to the world,
deliver me by this Thy most holy Body and Blood from all my sins and from all evils ;

make me cleave always to Thy commandments,
and permit me never to be separated from Thee, who, Thyself God, livest and reignest with the same God the Father and the Holy Ghost, world without end. Amen.

The 2nd prayer alludes to the letter of St. Paul to the Corinthians : « He that eateth and drinketh unworthily, eateth and drinketh judgment to himself, not discerning the body of the Lord » (I Cor. XI, 29). Several of them, indeed, « had suffered evils or even death » as a result of having « eaten the Lord's Supper » while profaning it by their pride, sensuality and contempt of their neighbour.

Perceptio corporis ... *Let not the partaking of Thy Body, O Lord Jesus Christ,*

which I, unworthy, presume to receive, turn to my judgment and condemnation ;

but let it by Thy mercy become a safeguard and remedy both for soul and body (Cf. Council of Trent, p. 67), *Who with God the Father, in the unity of the Holy Ghost, livest and reignest God for ever and ever. Amen.*

Taking the Host, the priest is inspired by the 13th verse of Psalm 115, and says :

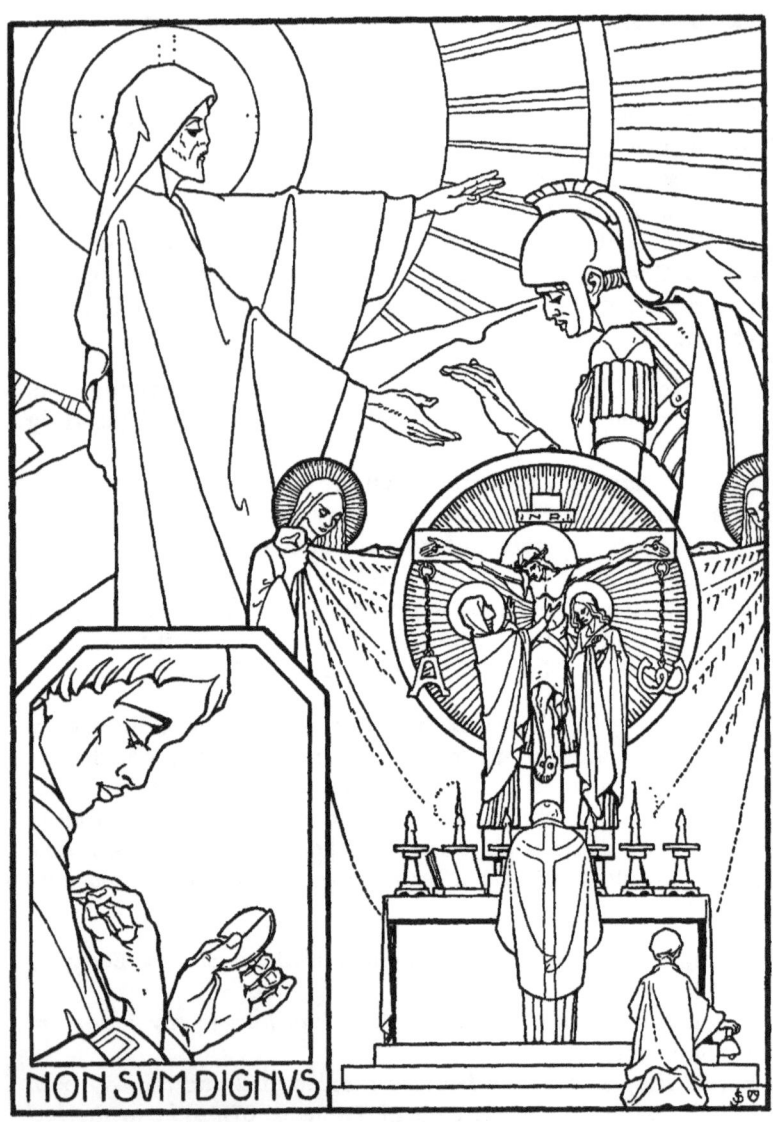

DOMINE, NON SUM DIGNUS: *(Top)* The Centurion says to Jesus: « Lord, I am not worthy that Thou shouldst enter under my roof; say but the word, and my servant shall be healed ». And Jesus replies: « Go, be it done unto thee according as thou hast believed ». — *(Altar and inset)* The priest holds in his left hand the Host, and with his right he strikes his breast saying three times the words of the Centurion. — The server rings the bell in order that everyone may unite in this action.

I will take the Bread of Heaven, and I will call upon the name of the Lord.

He then says three times, striking his breast *(see inset)*, the words of the Centurion whose humility and faith Jesus admired and rewarded *(top picture)* :

Domine non sum dignus ... *Lord, I am not worthy that thou shouldst enter under my roof ; but only say the word and my soul shall be healed.*

« When you eat the Body of the Lord », says Origen, the Lord enters under your roof. Therefore you, too, must humble yourself, and imitating the Centurion, say « Lord, I am not worthy... » (Hom. V in Div. loca Evang.). And St. Chrysostom : « Let us say to our Redeemer : Lord, I am not worthy that Thou shouldst enter into the house of my soul, but nevertheless, since Thou desirest to come to us, and encouraged by Thy mercy, we approach Thee » (Hom. de S. Thom. ap.).

In receiving the Host, the priest crosses himself with it, and says :

May the Body of our Lord J. C. preserve my soul unto life everlasting. Amen.

He purifies the paten saying the verses 12 and 13 of Ps. 115 and v. 4 of Ps. 17 :

Quid retribuam ... *What shall I render to the Lord for all the things that He hath rendered for me ?*

I will take the chalice of salvation and I will call upon the name of the Lord.

Praising, I will call upon the Lord, and I shall be saved from my enemies.

In taking the precious Blood, he makes the sign of the cross with the chalice and says :

May the Blood of our Lord J. C. preserve my soul unto life everlasting. Amen.

For the Communion of the faithful, the rite of the Communion of the sick was introduced into the Mass in the 13th Century. Thus the *Confiteor* is repeated (see p. 11). Then the priest holds up the Host, saying the words of the Baptist (see p. 105) :

Ecce Agnus ... *Behold the Lamb of God, behold Him who taketh away the sins of the world.*

The people strike their breasts 3 times saying with the faith and humility of the Centurion :

CORPUS DOMINI : *(Top)* Christ gives to His Apostles the bread and wine which He has transubstantiated into His Body and Blood. — *(Altar and inset)* Having given Holy Communion the priest purifies the chalice with wine, and his fingers with wine and water, saying two prayers which symbolize the purification and the lasting and internal effects of this passing and external Sacrament. — The server moves the missal from the Gospel to the Epistle side.

Domine non sum dignus ... *Lord, I am not worthy that Thou shouldst enter under my roof ; but only say the word and my soul shall be healed (dic verbo :* by thy word*).*

Placing the Host on the tongue of each communicant, the priest says :

May the Body of our Lord Jesus Christ preserve thy soul unto life everlasting.

The Last Supper was the prelude to «the marriage supper of the Lamb » of which St. John speaks (Apoc. XIX, 9). After eating the Paschal Lamb, the Apostles ate, in fact, the true Lamb of God, for Jesus offered Himself as Victim to His Father when he consecrated the bread and wine and gave them to them *(see top picture)* saying : « *Take ye and eat : This is My body. Drink ye all of this. For this is My blood of the New Testament* » (Mat. XXVI, 26-28).

Through the successors of the Apostles, this table of the sacrificial banquet which reconciles men with God is set up throughout the world. The Pope, upwards of 3.000 Bishops and 350.000 priests say Mass daily all over the world, from the rising of the sun in Asia and Oceania, and thence in Europe and Africa and the two Americas (see map, p. 64). All the faithful who so desire may daily eat at this Holy Table. And in partaking of the Victim Who is offered unceasingly that the Godhead may look favourably on them, they obtain the grace of an incorporation or vital union becoming ever more intimate with their divine Head and his whole mystical Body the Church.

« The sacrament of the Eucharist, a wonderful and living likeness of the Church — since the bread which is consecrated, formed of many grains, makes but one whole *(Didache 9, 4)* — gives us », says Pius XII, « the very Author of sanctifying grace so that through him we may obtain the spirit of charity which makes us live no longer our own life but the life of Christ and in every member of his social Body love the Redeemer himself » *(Mystici Corporis).*

« He who offers a sacrifice, says St. Thomas, should participate in it, for the exterior sacrifice which is offered is the sign of the interior sacrifice by which one offers oneself to God. In partaking of the Body and Blood of the Victim in Communion, the priest shows that the sacrifice is made interior for him » (III Q. 83 art. 4).

Jesus gives us His Body and Blood under the appearances of bread and wine, which are food and drink, in order to symbolize a vital association with His Passion and all the joyful, sorrowful and glorious mysteries which have their source in it. In receiving Communion we are, then, born together with Jesus to a new life, attaching ourselves as one with Jesus on the Cross, and living together with Him as risen from the dead and having « our citizenship in Heaven » (Phil. III, 20). This putting off of the old Adam, and putting on of the new Adam is the especial fruit of the Mass, for it is one and the same with Calvary ; at the prayer of the Church descends upon the altar and into our hearts « the living Bread », that is : the risen Christ, with all the mortifying and revivifying effects of His mysteries.

The Communion which is the completion of this sacred action entirely fulfils, therefore, the wish that Jesus expressed in instituting the Eucharist : « *In nobis unum sint.* As Thou, Father, art in Me and I in Thee, that they also *may be one in us* » (John XVII, 21). At this moment, above all, we are united with the divine life in recognising and loving, with Jesus, God as Father; and being, with Jesus, known and loved by the Father as His beloved children : « Father, said Christ, at the end of His discourse at the Last Supper, I have made known Thy name to them and will make it known, that the love wherewith Thou hast loved Me may be in them and I in Them » (John XVII, 26).

50. ABLUTIONS.

The priest then purifies the chalice with wine. Let us unite ourselves with his prayer :

Quod ore ... *Grant that what we have taken with our mouth, we may receive with a pure mind ; and from a temporal gift, may it become to us an eternal remedy.*

He washes his fingers with wine and water *(see inset)* saying:

Corpus tuum ... *May Thy Body, O Lord, which I have received, and Thy Blood which I have drunk, cleave to my inmost parts ;* (that is — to all the faculties of my soul) *and grant, that no stain of sin may remain in me* (see inset) *whom these pure and holy sacraments have refreshed. Who livest and reignest for ever and ever. Amen.*

51. COMMUNION ANTIPHON. — 52. POSTCOMMUNION. 53. ITE MISSA EST. — 54. PLACEAT. — 55. BLESSING.

See illustration, p. 114.

After the Communion (which is a verse of the Psalm which used formerly to be sung during the actual distribution of the Holy Eucharist) the priest greets the congregation with the *Dominus vobiscum*, which has its full significance at the moment of Holy Communion ; then he says the *Postcommunion*.

St. John tells us that the Angels and Saints in Heaven never cease to give honour and praise and thanksgiving to Almighty God, Who is seated upon the throne, and to the Lamb Who has redeemed all mankind with His Blood (Apoc. IV and V). In every Mass, throughout the whole world, their song is echoed, acclaiming the Father in the *Sanctus* and Jesus Christ in the *Benedictus*.

This hymn of triumph reaches its climax at the Consecration, which is the heart of the Eucharist. « When you see », writes St. Chrysostom, « the Lord lying immolated and the priest standing over the sacrifice and praying, are you not forthwith carried up to Heaven ? » (De Sac. l. III c. 4).

At the Communion all this worship of thanksgiving becomes more than ever our own, because the Divine Lamb is laid upon the altar of our own hearts and incorporates us in a more living union with Him. Thus our own thanksgiving is taken up into His own *(see top picture)* and becomes infinitely glorifying to God. This is the meaning of the *Postcommunion*, where we address God « through Jesus Christ our Lord », Who is truly present within us. « Christ », says St. Augustine, prays for us, as our Priest ; Christ prays in us, as our Head ; Christ is prayed to by us, as our God ». Thus we do not only thank the Lamb of God for having saved us and for continuing to do so in His Eucharist, but by Him, with Him and in Him, (all together, because He binds us all to Him in the bonds of His divine Love), we proclaim that He to Whom we owe all, and Who is The Lord, God, all powerful, is worthy to receive glory and honour and power, because by His Will all things have being and have been created (Cf. Apoc. IV, 11). This act of thanksgiving takes up the oblation of oursel-

POSTCOMMUNION — BLESSING: *(Top)* Christians, more and more incorporated by Holy Communion into a life-giving union with Christ, Who is the great High Priest and the Head of the Church, offer by Him, with Him and in Him their praise and thanksgiving to God the Father. — *(Altar)* The priest says the Communion and the *Postcommunion*, on the Epistle side: the *Dominus vobiscum, Ite missa est* and *Placeat* at the middle of the altar; then he blesses the people *(inset)* by making over them the sign of the Cross.

ves and of our whole lives into union with that which Christ, on the altar and in the highest Heavens, makes of Himself and of His Mystical Body, to His Father, from Whom all things come and to Whom all must return. « And when », says St. Paul, « all things shall be subdued unto Him, then the Son also Himself shall be subject unto Him that put all things under Him, that God may be all in all » (I. Cor. XV, 28). Each Mass and each Holy Communion begins and intensifies this complete surrender of our souls, which glorifies Christ and His Father, and ensures our eternal joy.

An Amen by the whole congregation should bring the fitting end to the Postcommunion which, like the Collect, is a *collective* prayer (see p. 36).

After another *Dominus vobiscum* the priest dismisses the congregation by the *Ite missa est* « You may go ». (The word « Mass » is derived from that « Missa »). At Masses for the Dead *Requiescant in pace* : May they rest in peace, is said instead.

The prayer which follows used to be called : *Prayer after Mass*, because it was said, together with the Last Gospel, by the priest in private. Hence the use of the expression « the homage of my bounden duty » which belongs to the priest alone (as in the *Hanc igitur*, p. 75, and the *Unde*, p. 83), because to him belongs the offering of the Holy Sacrifice, on his own behalf (*mihi*) and on that of the faithful (*omnibus*).

« **Placeat** ... *May the homage of my bounden duty be pleasing unto Thee, O holy Trinity, and grant that this sacrifice which I have offered all unworthy in the sight of Thy Majesty, be received by Thee and win forgiveness from Thy mercy for me and for all those for whom I have offered it. Through Christ our Lord. Amen* ».

The priest kisses the altar and gives the final *Blessing (inset)*, in the name of the God in Three Persons Whom the sacrifice has glorified and made merciful to us.

« **Benedicat vos** ... *May Almighty God bless you, Father, Son and Holy Ghost* ».

THE LAST GOSPEL: *(Top)* St. John the Evangelist writing his Gospel. Eagle-like, he scales the heights of the heavens and speaks of the eternal generation of the Word and of His Incarnation. He tells us that St. John the Baptist is God's witness to all men. — *(Altar and inset)* The priest reads the Last Gospel: *In the beginning was the Word*, making a cross on the altar, and genuflecting when saying: *And the Word was made Flesh*. All answer together: *Deo Gratias*.

56. LAST GOSPEL (St. JOHN)

Holy Communion, by making us participate fully in the sacrifice of the Mass, which is the continuation of the sacrifice of the Cross, enriches us with all the fullness of the fruits of the redemption. Thus we are freed through it more and more from all that hinders our path towards God, and put in a state of perfect dependence on Him Whom we glorify : we recognize in Him the Principle of everything ; we find in Him, too, our final Goal. He is the one and only Source of the *Life which is Divine*, the only *Truth and true Light* for our intelligence, the only and supreme *Happiness*, sole *Authority* and *transcendent Majesty*, infinitely adorable, for our wills.

The supreme fruit of the redemption is Jesus Himself, for that divine grace which is in our souls, that faith which is in our minds and that charity which, together with hope, is in our wills, unites us to the Son of God and admits us by Him, with Him and in Him to the Bosom of the Father. « We have seen and do bear witness and declare unto you the life eternal which was with the Father and which hath appeared to us, that... our fellowship may be with the Father and with His Son, Jesus Christ ». (I Joh. I, 2-3). Thus, engrafted living into the humanity of the Incarnate Word, we go to God. Therefore, the glorification of God as our Father, by our union in the bonds of the Spirit of love with His well-beloved Son, is the aim of the whole work of the redemption, concentrated in the sacrifice of the Upper Room and of Calvary, continued on every altar, and consummated gloriously in Heaven.

So, at Holy Communion (which is an integral part of the Holy Sacrifice) does the Son of God Himself come to us. Then the Church bids us read that Gospel where St. John shows us that He Who was born from all eternity of the Father was made Flesh ; and in receiving Him with faith and love (the Eucharist being the supreme means) we take part in His divine Sonship : « ex *Deo nati sunt* ».

It is by the Word that all has been made, because He is the Thought by Which the Father has conceived all things ; it is by the Word made Flesh that all has been re-made, especially through Holy Communion.

His forerunner leads us all to Him because it is his actual words which are used to tell us that the Lamb of God is in the Eucharist (see top picture).

In principio erat Verbum ... *In the beginning was the Word,*
and the Word was with God,
and the Word was God.
The same was in the beginning with God.
(The relation of the Word to humanity).
All things were made by Him
and without Him was made nothing that was made.
In Him was life,
and the life was the light of men,
and the light shineth in darkness,
and the darkness did not comprehend it.
(Sinful mankind rejected the truth).
There was a man sent from God
whose name was John.
This man came for a witness,
to give testimony of the light,
that all men might believe through him.
He was not the light, but was sent to give testimony of the light.
That was the true Light,
which enlighteneth every man
that cometh into this world.
He was in the world,
and the world was made by Him,
and the world knew him not.
He came unto His own (i. e. to the Jewish race)
and His own received Him not.
But as many as received Him,
He gave them power
to be made the sons of God,
to them that believe in His name :
who are born, not of blood,
nor of the will of the flesh, nor of the will of man,
but of God.
And (for) the Word was made flesh
and dwelt among us,
and we saw his glory,
the glory as it were of the only-begotten of the Father,
full of grace and truth.

57. PRAYERS AFTER MASS. — DEPARTURE.
See illustration, p. 120.

After the Last Gospel, the priest, kneeling upon the steps of the altar, says three *Hail Mary's*, a *Salve Regina*, two *prayers*, and a threefold *invocation to the Sacred Heart*.

These prayers are only said at low or « private » Masses, *in missis privatis*, and may be omitted when these have a certain degree of solemnity, such as : Masses with a sermon ; Masses at which a First Communion is made ; nuptial or burial Masses, or followed by Benediction or Exposition of the Blessed Sacrament (Decree of June 20, 1913).

These prayers had their origin from the days of Popes Pius IX and Leo XIII. The former ordered the recitation of one *Our Father* and one *Hail Mary* after Mass, to beg that the sad state of affairs brought about by the occupation of Rome might cease. The latter prescribed the prayers actually said now (that to the Blessed Virgin in 1884, to St. Michael in 1886), so that, thanks to the intercession of the Mother of Jesus « Who with her virginal foot shall crush the serpent's head » (Cf. Gen. III, 15), and of the Prince of that Heavenly Army « Who cast down into Hell the dragon and his angels» (Cf. Apoc. XII, 9), the fiendish persecution which had broken out with redoubled fury and malice might be brought to nought. In 1904, Pope Pius X authorized the invocation to the Sacred Heart.

Since the time when the « Godless » of Russia began with even greater pride and violence their campaign to destroy both priests and religion, Pius XI ordered that all these prayers should be said with the intention of diverting the evil that Satan was working through these men. « As I live », saith the Lord God, « I desire not the death of the wicked, but that the wicked turn from his way and live » (Ezech. XXXIII, 11) ; and the *prayer* implores God, through the merits of Jesus Christ *(per eundem Christum Dominum)* and « by the intercession of the glorious and immaculate Virgin Mary, Mother of God, of St. Joseph her spouse, of the Holy Apostles Peter and Paul, and of all the saints, *(see top picture)* in mercy and goodness (to) hear our prayers for the conversion of sinners and for

PRAYERS AFTER MASS: *(Top picture and altar)* The Saints, invoked by the priest in the prayers said kneeling at the foot of the altar: the Mother of God; St. Michael the Archangel, who routs the evil spirits from around the Church of God and « defends us in the day of battle »; St. Joseph, St. Peter, St. Paul and all the Saints. — *(Inset)* The priest leaves the altar, saying the hymn of thanksgiving of the three Hebrew boys in the furnace: *Trium puerorum,* with versicles and reponses, and three prayers, of which one is addressed to the martyr, St. Laurence.

the liberty and exaltation of our Holy Mother the Church, *pro libertate et exaltatione sanctae Matris Ecclesiae* ».

The prayers said at the foot of the altar do not form part of the Liturgy of the Holy Sacrifice. This accounts for the fact why, contrary to the prayers during the Mass itself, the priest addresses the Blessed Virgin and St. Michael direct ; also he kneels (even in Paschal-time) for the *Salve Regina*, and to say a prayer *(see picture of altar opposite)*.

This should help us to realize what are the special intentions which the Church, now that in our own era there is an open warfare against God, wishes us to interweave with our thanksgivings ; and as a means of doing so, to bear in mind the very special power which, « by Divine gift », Our Lady and St. Michael have against the forces of evil.

Without question, Jesus is our sole Mediator and Advocate before God ; but all the members of the Mystical Body are joined with the actions of their Head, and most especially those chosen vessels who are the « Mother of mercy, our advocate, *Mater misericordiae, Advocata nostra* », and that Archangel who, says St. Jude (Epist. 9) triumphed over the devil by the quiet threat : « May God rebuke thee : *Imperet illi Deus* ».

Trium puerorum. — The priest, united to the High Priest of all created things, Whose homage is infinitely pleasing to God, recites as he leaves the altar the *Song of the three young men*, which gives its true fullness to his thanksgiving. *(See inset)*. The three Hebrew boys, guarded by an angel, came unharmed through the flames and called upon all living things to praise the Lord with them. The pictures in the Catacombs often show this scene in the rooms where the Holy Sacrifice was offered. The triumphant joy of these young men typifies that of all the martyrs, of all those who have been witnesses for Christ, and from thence that of all Christians, whose daily life, intimately united to the Mass through Holy Communion, is a perpetual and faithful witness offered to God in union with the great Witness, or Martyr, of the Cross.

END.

Printed in Belgium by E. Vercruysse-Vanhove, St. Andries-near-Bruges.

www.ingramcontent.com/pod-product-compliance
Lightning Source LLC
Chambersburg PA
CBHW021012090426
42738CB00007B/757